Enemies

SJ Fowler is a poet, artist, martial artist and vanguardist. He works across poetry, sonic art, visual art, installation and performance, has published five books and been commissioned by the Tate, Mercy, and the London Sinfonietta. He is the poetry editor of 3:AM magazine, founder of the Maintenant series and curator of the Enemies project.

sjfowlerpoetry.com
weareenemies.com

Enemies

The Selected Collaborations
of SJ Fowler

Penned in the Margins

LONDON

PUBLISHED BY PENNED IN THE MARGINS
22 Toynbee Studios, 28 Commercial Street, London E1 6AB, United Kingdom
www.pennedinthemargins.co.uk

First published 2013

Printed and bound in the UK by Short Run Press Ltd., Exeter

ISBN
978-1-908058-13-3

CONTENTS

INTRODUCTION

We're born alone, we live alone, we die alone. Only through our love and friendship can we create the illusion for the moment that we're not alone.
Orson Welles

First and foremost, this book is a record of friendships. It is a testament to my refusing to be alone in the creative act, as I would not want to be alone in the world, and to my decision to mediate sociality through the artistic impulse of other human beings, whose brilliance leaves me feeling more at home in that world. If my daily life is primarily defined by individuals who have decided to make their brief time on this planet one of creativity, ingenuity, intelligence and humour, and who have talents far surpassing my own, my experience of life can only be one that is defined by constant growth and learning and, hopefully, understanding — towards nothing more than more art unto expiry. Maybe even enough to temporarily blot out life's adversarial character and essential purposelessness. Certainly it has worked recently, and that's more than enough for me.

This is why the book exists as selected collaborations, whittled down from over 60 different exchanges I have been a part of over the last few years with writers, poets, artists, photographers, illustrators, designers, sculptors and filmmakers from across the world. The act of collaboration has become a defining turn in my practice, a constant affirmation of a way of writing as well as a way of communicating in real space, between human beings.

Enemies is a record of potentiality too, of what the aberrant and ambiguous use of language can be when responding, warping and enveloping another, equally abundant, artistic medium. It is my view that poetry lends itself to collaboration as language does conversation, and it is in poetry we are renovating the living space of communication, and this in itself is a collaborative act. The poet comes up against something other than themselves in the writing of every poem; and in the shaping of every fragment of language there is a response taking place. I hope this book showcases original, dynamic examples of what is produced when the other in question is the equally avid mind of another artist or writer.

The motivation behind my taking on so many collaborations was initially a source of uncertainty for me. I've come to realise this reluctance (I began collaborating by invitation, the Voiceworks and Blue Touch Paper projects being early examples) is intensely important. It's becoming clearer with time that I undertake so many collaborations precisely because, at heart, I believe less than many of my peers in the transformative power of poetry. That isn't to say I believe poetry isn't transformative at all — of course I do ascribe it such potential (to me personally, it is utterly and immensely transformative — but I refuse it the power to go beyond my own personal subjectivity. I refuse the idea that poetry is improving in and of itself. There is a tension here, maybe even a paradox. I have both feelings at once, that poetry is both nothing and everything. Yet I do believe, somehow and without articulation, in the Brodskyite notion of poetry being the most important artform because of its relationship to the profundity of language, because of its engagement with what fundamentally constitutes all other creativity and discussion. It is impossible for me to escape the feeling that this relationship is wholly individuated, and so at the very same moment — poetry is nothing, a game for the initiated, the distraction of a select. I suppose then that my poetry, and my collaborations, are about stripping away a glib assumption that poetry is profound, to get to the private meaning, which I do believe is utterly closed and personal though very much present. Here is the second paradox: by maintaining a creative practice often reliant on an other, and an act of exposure toward them, I am able to gain fresh and invaluable access to my own poetry and its process. Paulo Friere's notion that communication builds community in the creative, organisational act which is the antagonistic opposite of manipulation, and a natural development of unity, ties into the idea that my collaborations might be founded on a central turn — a paradox of dismissiveness and legitimacy about the poetical act and the nature of poetry's power. For me then, this book is a confusion as well as a testament, a symbol of community and accord, as well as a record I cannot fathom on re-reading. And this is exactly how it seems to me it should be — lost in the margins.

Artists who are powerful alone, and need not collaborate, seem to do so easily, uninterested in the protection of their inspiration. If this book is held together by poetry, it is as a soft and tacky kind of glue — uhu — as good for eating as for adhesion, barely keeping pace (which is its strength, I hope, that it acknowledges this in its very firmament) with the photography, art, illustration, musical composition and design of so many gifted others to be found within these pages. I have been told it is a book dense and mysterious, full of challenging material, and shifts in tone. It doesn't seem so to me, nor did it feel so in its multifarious creation or compilation. But then perhaps that is because I hope that if my work stands for one thing, it is that experimentation and innovation is not a stance, but a pattern of behaviour, not a philosophy of theory, heavy with beneficial and smug associations of rebellion and kudos, but a specific reaction to a specific need or notion — a philosophy in action. How might I express what I wish to outside of atypical methods? This I do not know, interested as I am in the untameable and almost unknowable, and the dark edges of experience, emotion, civilisation and its history. Broken syntax, free verse, Oulipian codas, found text, unconscious writing, high conception &c.: these are what I deem the necessary tools and, as I hope will be clear throughout this volume, ones wholly symbiotic with the subject of each collaboration and the work of each collaborator.

The twenty-nine works ahead of you are almost always excerpts from larger works. At the end of the book you will find a Notes section, which will shed some light on the content and process of each collaboration, and where you'd find them in their full length, if relevant. I want to thank all the collaborators who made it into the book, all those who didn't, probably better off not being associated with me, and Tom Chivers, editor of Penned in the Margins, who does important work, selflessly and with immense professionalism. Special debts of gratitude to Jon Opie and Shonagh Manson at the Jerwood Charitable Foundation, who, alongside Arts Council England, have allowed the concept for this book to grow into a huge programme of events and undertakings involving over thirty happenings and two hundred artists and poets. And to David Kelly and Livia Dragomir, monsters who cannot be unmentioned.

Consider this meagre work in your hands a rather miniaturised bulwark against being solitary — a sandcastle before a tsunami, that might provide you with the smallest apertures of pleasant distraction. For my own part, if my work sits alongside, or inside, work of a quality such as I hope you will find beyond this page, it can only be elevated. The others who are my Enemies in art and in life, who make up my community, and who will not let me be complacent, are what this book means to me. I hope for you it might take on another meaning that I cannot possibly fathom from my privileged vantage.

— *SJ Fowler*

Enemies

The Mechanical Root
w/ Emily Critchley

what isn't abandonable...
it sounds / the baby plays
like the tune that
to do your worst / best
going over the water
what isn't unconscionable
may be very lovely
in a London twilight
like the clinging of stone
onto yr vine / out of traffic
towrd spring
where plans []
have very
& start sprouting
in a field of vision
crazy! out of vision
the cut & rub
all things
& were it up to us
we'd happily watch everything
we'd built burn
only the newer will know
peace from this
rustling
in conference season:
something that's passed around
like a drink
... cover ears
the mood will pass
& I know I know
myself

to sleep about that child
without the money
the worry of that
& other things
advancing — like
to be in this world,
only out of it.
The next day
is sometimes / terrifying
stretching outward
for our babies
what value may come
from propagating
more ends / more
abundances in scarcity
this part the cast
of birds that buzz
the cat / I enjoy
seeing the water
life with A woman
the new part
revealing / possible
hang of heart / home
a fw months older than
the Pope which hasn't
rust to make
about it / she wants
to love as low baby
broken nose / grows
a few softer words?

Museum of Debt
w/ Alexander Kell

you can get a sudden attack of nausea by staying too long in an art gallery as well. It must be some kind of illness — museumitis — unknown to medical science. Or could it be the air of death surrounding all things man-made, whether beautiful or ugly
> *Gustav Heyrink*

i. what a strange illusion it is to suppose beauty is goodness

> wife; lunatic
> until moonlit
> then, a dwarf
> of melody
> a celestial harmony
> perfection
> below
> thus, a debut
> in the unter
> tow

ii. tooth of the Nile

ark of the covenant
baby hercule
as asp, a thesp
a guided tour
of softcore

iii. swimming the river Birkenhead dry

Cuckoo, witness my record
3 in a day
& fights won between
a life tired
to temper hard to soft
mean to kind
but always open pursed
friends, there are shadows
in any case

vii. Anna O

in the number
zero
fishmouth
blindness
every woman
dies alone

viii. Saint Christopher ponders the desert

      the salt of the salt mouth
      will my maid be plucked
      in heaven? or virtuous?
      I'd prefer to clean myself,
      if the help aren't sluts
      for time is short.
      suicide machine on the crow's nest
      I look upon the lip to see
      the gardener himself is soon to mulch
      ash me instead! I'd not be ratfed

ix. Jessica cannot hide what lies beneath

sweat sticky lotus
   licked
  the young fox hides its tail
  it protects a secret
    shaped like a cashew nut

        12 bars
      the rhythm   method
        fails

                  again

x. an air Charles Whitman

urban monk practises, both light for new fight
the gun, the worry, the heavy securita
those usual visitors at my back gate
how familiarity has killed divinity
they used to knock
before entering, now
a trigger, back and to the left
to offer rest for the hand
from which the moon leaks
to reload! happily, a sighted family ready to stop hot police
for the last kind minutes falling like pollen
a Noh drama of assassins — on the bowels of doubt I ride
a bad pronounced words today
all forever, work here into dead kids

xi. Mountaineer

He had spent so many useless hours with others.

Ingeborg Bachmann

> I see flowers
> in dead space
> where banana's grow
> thirty five late nights
> clouds fall, sickness longs
> I swap freedoms for moneys
> … either way, soon I return
> to morning, sober like a spider
> where a mere fud cannot reach me

xv. Primae Noctis

a cry of birth, a challenge
to change a lightbulb
hipping in Falkirk, the detective
one misery lets go
like fingers uncurling
from a branch
the dream in room four;
a crippled woe'd beggard approaches
gastric, palsy overload
& new nearly saint
wisdomed, he asks for you

xviii. Saint Christopher enters the desert

& out of the building there was no more building
no homes & little in the way of kindnesses
just huddled together for warmth

hardwords & poverty
thick varicosal veins says one
& wonder why, in the long of the blue flower
there is no mention it will soon be gone

dogfights, breathing heavy with all that muzzle
is to remain in life for soon enough anyhow…
you will become
'suspended'

xxii. Apostasy

look at this fate, this is a human recourse
there are pits to dig
a Russian dance of Travelodge boredom
there will be suicides;
a sadness no one addresses
mental health is our new canteen
salut to the artist / worker
he is the soil in which hope is grown
wait for a minute… violins, a march
its 1984, the urn is strong
I smell petrol, & finally after so many
thousand false starts
this abandoned bag turns out to be explosive

xxvii. the fat duck is worth every penny

precisely because the wind did I run at lunchtime...

my hands so blue they could no longer
close into mitts
to be fit! to have abs so I can buttfuck a choirboy
without conscience or worship
I humbly kneel before my pope ... joan
a grape becomes a pellet for princess
a dropbox private video for Norwich
a straw dot upon the forehead, a red piñata
& a glass black eye smartly adorned
with my image, approaching, smartly
a camera - what has been witnessed
in the ford centre, upon the orange
a fury prawn charging at a pig's eye
boys & dancing choose

xxviii. the 77 lives of Jahangir Robinson

of Henri Bergson's theory of time
what living wage
exists, finer,
when not following a crime?
slow at wanting fast
fast at wanting slow
dribbling into the subjective perception of each minute

xxix. *wrack of the Nile*

the pantheon of western diseases abound
fatigue, arrhythmia, angina ... cancer
antichrist in gallery weave, black spider
two clowns docking, drinking blood
a desire to charge one's phone
before the Rosetta stone
& a root cause, watching stephen king's 'it'
numbers, himmed, then barred
then hammered through the shitbox
of an essex lattice, the false
attachment — a radio that rots waves
a really, really bad diet
for the suspects usual invading
we will be revenged up the left shoulder
by pickpockets in their millions

xxx. Cherry Cola / Screaming Eagle

When a man enters his thirtieth year, people don't stop calling him young.

Ingeborg Bachmann

the butterfly is fruiting the plank
sent forth in the form of freckles
but the equal eagle is permanent
a mammal bird beating her love
a soul to accompany her spirit
with hot blood the body is her spirit
but bacterium is sheer
technician of her eternity
it is no accident the symbol
of nations is winged, pampered
ready to splay weight across gravity

xxxi. maximym securitii black dolphin

golden scorpions crawl from the cunts of majorettes
signifying the beauty of death under the jewelled belts
and threatening those who refuse to see it
> Robert Mezey

the tiger panting
in a painting
the blue dolphin
turned black
the white swan
shudders
risking becoming alone
it is hard to get behind
another portrait of hot Stalin

I'm sorry I didn't let you enjoy it

Gilles de Rais
w/ David Kelly

the magician television show which isn't true to life .

this is the best of all says prelati
mixing tobbacco
too many fish in the sea apparently
to keep
the quench clenched
oh well no use in crying
now 30 years or 300 years later unless there's
some hard money involved
but I am not able
to forget, Gilles in drowning
in his dreaming
of the happy society kissed as a king

shot in the ribs in revenge .

my organs like this, two ribs, rhymes
and emily's
racist baby workout
is a future collected book
like this a postcard sized box that is completely
empty as a hospital bed
can be empty soon
enough if you don't watch your mouth & if so
I'll be on quick as a flash
evidence for it in my past

it was awkward before it was over .

all of my friends are dead — too bad for them
Bruce Andrews

& it was hard out there & there was
clap of thunder
oh & mary were we are not friends
hands up says Gilles
I admit it, truth be
told I don't know why I did it maybe because
I enjoyed it, maybe I mean are you going?
its not as though I killed that many children?
is it just because sex is involved? he asked
for I killed far more of the young on the battlefield

who remembers Biafra ?

young wars are paid for by being cherished
the older ones
are so sick of war because it is
behind them so what do they do for hobby
when they have all
this free time on their hands
after well they round up all the children of the
village lands
and these are happenings and there's
a depression apparently but that doesn't seem
an excuse to me but I've not been where you are

jacob wrestling the angel .

jacob wrestling the angel & it got really dark
taking hold, under the gooks: 50 / 50
they wrestled to death
now there are too many images
when the commission fails
to resolve the difficulties
and to resolve the allegations
my ankle sprained when I ran to check
the windows were locked before we
went away for a really long time
to China, or Turkey, or some prison
in the unlikely event
of using the escape slide
it spins

meditations on violence .

*I hear their footsteps or their voices in the depths of the galleries of stone and I run
with joy in search of them*
        Jorge Luis Borges

digging up the dead he said for there is
safety in the workhouse
for first taught Gilles
avoidance, be sensitive to the threat
unencounter
it then escape
if you run then do run away from me
then dissuasion, dissuade me from the red wings
to the green dog of france
a spear in Lille
for it to leave before finally action with artifice
no entree, whole vehemence & awful distruction

bricked inside a royal's pardon .

across the pretty one
an urchin, in the sea
monkey is a Dragon bad
until love takes fold
unites into one being
the tail & nose of a seahorse
captured alive
whose names are memorable like an acid bath etching of the
victory in the underpants?
friends to all
& all over the evacuation
in order to you something tall
because we're very famous

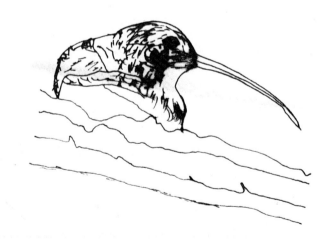

awake to a world ashamed .

Everybody's mouth
is somewhere else, I know, somebody's anus
I speak a mystery, only to you
Here's all my blood in pawn.
  John Berryman

silly moon overheard
it doesn't bode well for the kiddles
on placed never said the little girl
little knowing the transformed
earth worm was not her friend in all of this
no joke to Gilles, the rest of her body
warm as the new
snapped her humur
it didn't look all that friendly we might
say, vein & poisonous as he'd say all ancient snakes are
Gilles with a magic
is shaking the tree

Ways of describing cuts
w/ Sarah Kelly

the Second off:
  docking in Essex, wondering how it ended
up like this, dogging
first in Epping forest, then scarred
brutalised, cheeky
in some abandoned farmhouse near the set
of Grange Hill...
actually I've confused you with someone else...
you both wear netball bibs

I wasn't there then, with my play
pleating at skirts
not at the beacon neither
because the bread of ovens held
stones sometimes
as we must not forget   that importance if
trunked trees part to
waylay our motives
                so dock leaves
don't green our whites
unless stung prior by pride

did you say trunked trees? I've
misheard again
a group of people who know each
other?
together, not forgetting
just saying a bunch of words together?
not forgetting
{like} nutrients sawdust masking circa moderate L.E.D. tocsin
just a lot of bullshit making me squirm?
no, this is
ballet
not a poetry
& you were in a skirt, I saw the ex's pride
alright, it was big

together, not regretting no
longer lustless and child-begun
your sentence again for you because
we needed it so
said and safe and nutritious
that soil licked from nails
prickles at our words
bunched up in
stalks string
how did the fuchsias decay?
because they were layed together and
knowing eachother?
skirts shrink and
ride in the dog dancing
what treasure doesn't scar
      and scold the tongue

the democratic republic of bears
allows for misery bears
for Oligarchs
for poles & ropes & cherry bears
pickling veins furry
like a morbid stucko angioplasty
bally balloon bally bear
   swim my lady poet
   swim vegetable Octopi
swim to bear down on us
 my long hair & the smoke of your pipe

picking phrases as fruits now,
two, three fours on all
floors how the red rushed off
the bairn inside
stomach scotched and
pickled by the
tobacco and the key
to the ornate gate
overgrown, I   resemble
       gardens
overthrown you
tear upon my patience
paw at me
I hold no lady upon no to poet
sufferance of caged animation, we
your smooth sucks of thunder rain
down upon bodily
parade
not a poetry
just a sitting and a speech

not a putty
answering questions with a question
why is Belladonna using her foot?
toes as feelings
as rubber ribs
new for us both
the risk of deep vein thrombosis
the burial seeds too deep to grow but there
is the concern birds will eat us
a gobble, a nosh or in Wales, a bach
a propaganda gift for your departure
take to them word of our damp
our softness
our squib
when it counts most
we fail to maintain our solidity

and arity as questions come and
argument solders us in this gifts of function
I, fear and so flee, in part, I think, to the woods
for the wood to augment our rocking chairs
the porch we talk upon and bird-listen
to the structure of the V solidarity meets at edges of
a communication
fished from across the Thames to a tango of membrane
sodden and film flimsy now
nests
I hold only the smoking end of the pipe

the bath
to the point of fainting
all mess of inspired
lightheaded
naked on the matt
emulsion
sat with carrot
small hands
heavy with knuckles of crack
& brittle bath for the kids
now for me
given
a free performance
but not
worth

a chest
nor trove
with pearlescence
of define and right
nocturnal
at the crack of the foot
on the crab on the
tile
slipping is never the
option we went toward
but as childlike our streetlighted corridor veins
could sever where the floorplan misdirected
lay it down here — your stand and say

one day there will be a Nuremburg
says you to Uki
says you landing
strip & natural
that a feast
meat on a bloated
puffy poppy
like the dread dancer
toe'd to meat again
steak
reminding you say
a real city on a real sea
Odessa might cuts

and stepped as
you are in your teeth-turn
playing the same rule
again & again
hushed for fewer
wish we could   eat
it all up
with the promise
perfectly in a piece
using my words
on your terrain
makes for the
cemetery a pass
over gusto — should
our travels always
reverse our times?

Art Gallery Bouncer
w/ Patrick Coyle

#9

dont go just another excuse to let 5 million more illegals in the country. Watch this space. even the athletes dont turn up and go awol. & Blimey - Only 8 white kids in the pic

#10

Pretty much every bit of individuals movie clip sexual web sites comprise a remarkable method of type of awesome adult substance, most of it bizarre and perverted shitting in public

#11

26 up, 8 down buy don't shit on your doorstep mugs, tshirts and magnets Don't sleep with your housemate or workmate, it will get messy! Bob wants to shag his PA but Fred told him "Don't shit on your doorstep"

#12

Then he told me that hes busy feeding his polar bear milk. This ladies and gentlemen proves my theory that animus lives in the north west of canada on an island actually closer to greenland than civlised canada, with his mother and his milk sucking polar bear. I dont really want to know what animus does with his polar bear in the evenings but im sure its disgusting. Beware of animus he will set his milk sucking polar bear on you who will feed on your nipples.

#13

Hi the my dear lonely person!!! My name is Ekaterina, I am 27 years old.. I live in Russia, in city Sochi. I search for the person who would understand me.. I want serious intentions, and serious relations.. I want to find love, I want to find good person with whom I can spend all my life.. If you are interested in me if you want to study about me more, write to me the letter at my e-mail mosmaryy@gmail.com ! Ekaterina !

#14
I didn't realize this was a dating site, I must have lost my site manual.

#15
Oct 19, 2007 ... I *Lost My Sight*, Not My Vision. If life's hard knocks have beat you up to the point that you rather give up here is a blueprint on how to ...

#16
Melanie and Thomas have gone out to eat and are deciding on what to order. Even though Melanie claims not to be so hungry, they still order a lot, because the dishes on the menu look too delicious.

#17
Tagged in post by *Patrick Coyle* Dirty *Egg* will be playing - it's a short comedy starring This is England's Perry Fitzpatrick, Thomas Turgoose and Chanel ...

#18
Steven Fowl offers a keen observation on the impact of the agenda driven approach to the text. "Much modern scholarly biblical criticism operates on the assumption that there is something hidden by or hidden inside the text. Moreover, the corollary of this assumption is that the properly trained critic is just the right person both to determine what this subject matter is and how to extract it from the text. [together]:

#19

This capacity is ideally become to an individual with demonstrated experience across buyer service, supply chain & logistics within a production environment where quality is high. Simply respond to this email to get more answers. Feel free to forward your Resume for a confidential discussion. They are looking forward to consider the job occasion with you.

#20

This work is ideally fit to an individual with demonstrated experience through purchaser service, supply chain & logistics within a production environment where quality is paramount. Simply respond to this email to find more information. Feel free to add your Resume for a confidential discussion. They are looking forward to talk over the job questions with you.

#21

I am aware that this is certainly an unconventional approach to starting a relationship. My Name is Ng Catherine

#22

The study has become shorter! 5-6 years later you were born you go to the school! Then you go to the college! Are you ready to study all life?

#23

Hyperlinks in emails come in two flavours - a) short, informative and to the point, or b) ugly.

#24

I'm Carmen Marin, passionate poetry and literature. I live in Romania, Europ. I am 37 years. I love journalism and music also.

#25
If you live in eupope just became a fun and you will see the foto album thera all the flags of europe, all the funs have the right to be tagged themself to the flag of there country.

#26
Anthony *Patrick Coyle* What's a little sex offense matter when it comes to love? ... Anthony*Patrick Coyle* I'm sticking with Plenty of Fish. ...

#27
"Phenonemally cruel," says Gawker. "Stephen Fowler is everything wrong with the elitist eurotrash transplants in this country," (Fowler is British) says Fixn' To. Anybody else have something to say?

#28
Remember *Patrice Coyle* from the past? Use the friend finder at MyLife™ to ...

#29 On behalf of my friend Lenore, I find some of them write rubbish, plus their spelling is atrocious.I had a few minutes to spare tonight,so I decided to post this comment.

#30
i live next to a santander employee, he is strange and nobody trusts him, hes been spotted urinating in his own back garden on several occasions and peeping through his curtains at night with a kiddies telescope.

Animal Husbandry
w/ Sian Williams

soon balljoints bur
        teeth chatter in the heat & marrow sneers
                a baby has fallen
        so what but cancer is closer to death
            than two skeletons
                    pummelling each other?

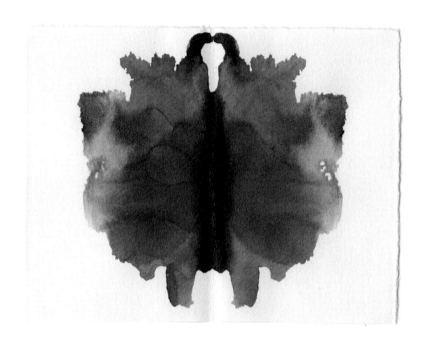

coral sponge
moisture partnered to a dead thing
a dog struck by a car nearby
& the reception is ruined
but still
born
red then on a   plane of red before the black bar

there are two cities
under one city all the dead are buried
they   the good ones
whittled eyes
I am from the other city

the descent seemed endless
we discovered the exemplary steps
& climbed down into those squalid rooms
                    speleologists charting caves
what we had been wailing for
the clear prints of two blood-stained hands

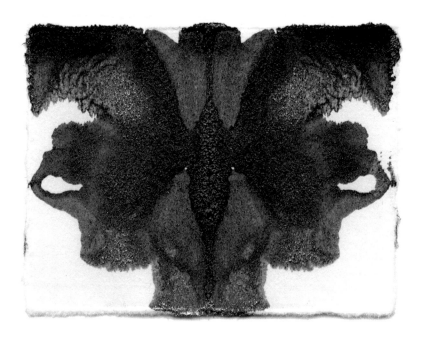

my mole does not fear death
      he can barely see it

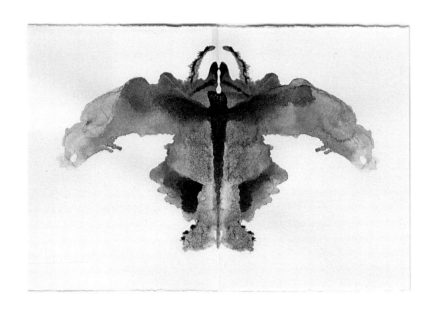

the site of birdsleeping
how beautiful to be received into sleep by your
side
but who wakes shattering day?
the crowns who clammer
your nipples cut circles in the water

eight girls
without underwear
barking like labradors

such is the result   of being carried
away

40 feet
w/ David Berridge

a mouth sewn sht by the early enemy of the mind
summer, sassoon david sassoon
the betters
the graph recording of a forest
the mountain push, the zooo
little girls who smoke and smoke
the cat in bill in vein
lectured till dawn
then ran toward and lectured were and sent

there was an old recording
an animal stuck in mud
a calling of that, then it's back to work, the first morning
in pain, and wishing then the point above was a spade
not a phonograph, made up stories

and this was the day a rothko was defaced
the soft bones of the city, made opera
once
I ruined you the spruce of the Swedish exfoliate
steep
ed performances and that early recording
of me juicing and juddering my tiny worn
out in grave
cy.warmth. ug. foreigned died.

a monstrous figure at rights drags a man
tied by his feet with a rope, the position
of his body and its whiteness contrasts
with the chaos of monsters, animals
and demented faces of these around him rendered in gray

what can I tell you about mud
to our fullest extent
in all directions glossed
Uncle's bewildering variety
the inches of his guffaw
are we elegiaicists
epigrammatists
off course
happy in our detumescence

is the red palace
for who in this and weeps

I'd Americanize trout

outer space is Ipswich
but up commuter lore
blood boils at Manningtree

without a suit
pledge to horizontal
today I will use my veto

why feign a rust
only the holy ghost

Rothko left the moon cull
some imaginary beings

goodnight night night see you in
    the pitch
sensuous god all the way through

pallbearers of floor thirteen
    always a funny story
    about the corpse in question
reservoirs of delinquent pandas
oiling at a certain temperature

now close the lid quipped Goliath
instructions WERE given on the
    phone

listen as the blooming of the doomed
animals ear into nethery syringes, neigh arts,
all knuckle, all night, were friends with mouth
for my friend, because she's about
& soon will not be

I leave behind Karl Kraus no longer in the mountains
for you & andy, are the spectral couple
who require a bear's maid, a classic tale
the ungrounded rider, horseless, on a broom
forcing me to go back to work
let's handhold the feast, sweatingtodeath in a dragon's mask

i feel sick toward my stomach
hower'd the day dies, not a new diet now
redrum, the fastest horse for a boss
not a new down, where certain set times
rob the kitternken of his breathing apparatus

nausea is not normal, listen to the body & his
synchronic back pain
his dada's help to get ready for school
north wind evening, early repetition, getting used to it early
putting out that lovely blue seal-flame
with a bucket of soil

the city things
stopped a while ago
is that a curlew? who   lazy Romans
am I asking? No one   seeking an image field
lives this slowly   a word pool
unless they are an earth   into which to dip
in revolt   7:32   on the far edge of

          locate the beast as being

white hope of the environ-   time without news
mental movement   to really work
shot a Wasabi down a straw   an anecdote
your Pisa   masticate it fully for
doesn't lean
huge meat pie in coat pocket

the indents
in your face once monks' fish ponds
windmill out of your ruinous mouth
into the armed City of London policeman's   if we don't exist
sushi box (the   beards and ships
                                              ships and beards

wasabi) drop of
sandalwood on each wrist

with aphorisms
I emerged from the toilet at French customs
the National Express bus had gone

dig holes and push

each other in `   run off
with fire
to indicate affection

still the happiness
of eating seafood
tiny wooden bloke

more than the death of Ceefax
I'm buying a St.George's flag

goose of perpignon which sprouts from the engine
of overpaid work
that is the slim chest of music
shaped like the tibetan curtain
if the herder
safety sees someone on the grasslands after dark
he is obliged to ride them
for there are wolves out
to there, you know

how to kill
travelling is words the society
remember to disseminate hard work, I warm you David
loneliness is inevitable
but the ...
can transform us into
our ideas we accordion
strangle it's air tree, which looks down upon the crowds
don't forget this is a ruthless
publish
the future depends on it

happy birthday lineliness is my water filter it nurtures me
inside the parcel you will find
a jar of kind beehoney and a bag of toenails
kiss your evil claws
and you smile now i see your goodness fangs
canines breeding horses in inner mongolia
strangling rabid dogs with that wise smile
be humble and courteous during your travels
look after yourself
remember your body belongs to the revolution

read standing up
in the kitchen after midnight
ethical and juridical
it's the bits about traveling
that make me cry the most

tuba I once played has returned to corner me in my grown man's
                                                        fear
soon one or both of us
mouthing above the noise of the writing machines
          house of tuna chunks
          tested with a spirit level
          everyone's an uncle
          original homemade fibrillator

inspiring a young Les Dawson
will claim evolution
stoic turkeys thought it was Easter
whilst the pods the
   little Emirates Airline pods
descend
   into North Greenwich
it feels like the seaside
on this particular Sunday
          maybe every Sunday
eyes closed the whole ride Sufi Master

                         yes I'm coming to live with you
                         on the door step with my suitcase
                         of your books like drinking
                         from holes in frozen lock water

The Rasenna
w/ David Kelly

because of the unseasonly heat
I don't care about the past
a gargoyle
with two noses
for each end of the flower
lying near the crumbling walls
I am a babe
suckling the moneymilk
of the knights templar
cheers to them

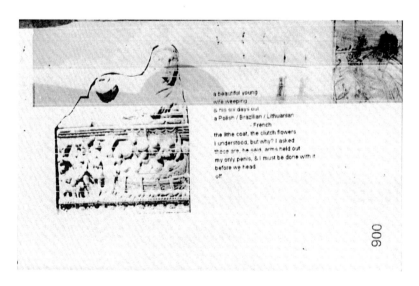

a beautiful young
wife weeping
& his six days out
a Polish / Brazilian / Lithuanian
- French
the lithe coat, the clutch flowers
I understood, but why? I asked
these are, he said, arms held out
my only penis, & I must be done with it
before we head
off

900

tugging her pasta alternatives
from the black ram
I realise we are loving
upon a rug
& shriek
my manhood has left me

& she calls me a 'girl'
just as I feared
the stonecold climate of growing up in Newquay

a love litter willing
to you
who risks widow
to pain supply crusade

so fresh
a fruit
sorry
you're so hardly even there
& may one day not be
untouched (what a
waste – I had waited all week
to say something beautiful
& instead
again
I am just left
pointing out the faults
of others.)

Secretum Meum
w/ Tim Atkins

BOOK II

{Saintly Augustine & the ever modeste
Francesco Petrarch are witnessed ambling
a julian alp with ease, their minds elsewhere,
deep in conversion...}

A. Have you achieved saturation?

F. Like a nappy, just enough to speak to you.

A. I have the talcum. Speak. Tell me everything.

F. Hold Onam inute! You say I boast of my speaking, as though I
could hold it in my hand, like a boy pearl... Well the only words
I claim is that I have never trusted it. Why should I be proud of
reading many books, from which I have derived little learning but
much distress of mind? You accuse me of seeking a town outside of
London in fancy language when, as you went and admitted when
jousting about the white puff powder, my chief torment is that my
books are Balham to your Collier, they are all like dusted, because
of the Talc, and not fatted, because of your kitchen. Burgers again,
isn't it? Can't suffice to express ideas, a bit of beetroot in with the
mince, as they say. And when you talked seriously about about my
beautiful hair, with the straightrazor line etched in by tattoo, you
almost made me laugh. Why are the hairdressers in my frogman's
with such bad hair? Why do they listen to trance music all day?
Renting their chairs like mercenaries... So I have put my hope in
this wretched mortal quiff, as it swishes over my face, which daily
warns me of its frailty? Heeu forbid! I admit that when I was a

pleasure in showing off my fine frame and licking down my hair, but such vanity disappeared with Thrones, episode one, season two! The book is called the Kings, it will be written, and mark my words, in two years, everyone will have this cut.

> A. Gene Thrones played baseball, if I recall rightly. Are you alluding to him? And why be cross? In my secret book appeared these initials. Did you explain them to me? In a toga? I was dreaming. When I look at your hair across the centuries I am thinking of becoming a vegetarian. I love your language, Francis. As much as this sandwich. Sing me something winning.

F. Were it so! Were it that I was as strong as you! Hear the crows north of the wall start croaking, wait until the wolves start to get into my answers. Like Lawrence, Kind of earthly Eigner, bound to my home like a tortoise. He pays the price for clear vision. I do not like to say what I have learned to say about able men, lest I should marrow my tongue with such harsh nasty harshness — "slowly   I have sometimes heard my nose click / as if some naked siftings bared themselves"

> A. And so, who, if any, is greater than Larry? The thing you're after / may lie around the bend / of the nest, even, he said (or how read it) / line after line // given one look // refresh the eyes / against the abyss. It is a buffoon who calls Walt Whitman rubbish just because he made some of it up. In the jacket of a rabbit!

F. Come on, I am not if anything avaricious, I don't care about what kind of chair I'm in, and I can't be absolved by training. This is not to say I don't heed your advice, it's just, if I am to not walk in footsteps because I cannot walk, I may as well wheel my own way.

> A. Yours is the list of a marble. Expertise in trousers is improved often by sucking. You must decide for yourself how many others you will enter for awards, but it is indubitable that in the whole population of your region, in which you are after all but one, there is such a poverty of language. Is the poem to be unlike a duck's ass and not admit to either opening or closing? This is not only the words as isolated monads, but their ordering. Empathy must have moderation, otherwise it dissolves distance and does away with itself. Everything should be taken for itself, but not too much, otherwise it's lost. Any wall — flat or curved — is just there standing up. I am not in it for the parking space — and despair is the worst of all evils. When I learned I would never be able to talk again, I was speechless.

F. I'm not inhuman enough to be unmoved by concern for my friends, especially those who are endeared to me by their virtue and merit. Some I admire, some I venerate, some I love, some I pity. On the other hand I'm not so high minded as to ruin myself for my friends - I have to think of my own future, provide a competence for old age, and hence combine some material concern with my cultivation of the muses. This is why I am the squatting poet... I mean with weights, weightlighting ... forget it ...

> A. ...Which strengthens the kidney — if you come up, slowly. For we must make a new world through a surfeit of the social. And — of course — love of language and love of each other. I wouldn't want to start a punch-up in an empty

room, although several in this spaceship would. The direct
observation & the direct thought, the language & its derive.
Well, that's the point, isn't it? — to a dead man in a toga.
How can one build a tepee out of concrete? Or an avant-
garde from an academy?

F. Humbly though I try to be it seems I keep emerging as hubly or
humby. I realise I am still childish, as a man, and as a poet because
my problem with those who start a punch over in an empty tent
like their fights metaphorical, or even worse, verbal, where as I
still like mine actual, and would happily join them in starting up
their cars if they really meant to ramraid each other, rather than
metaphorically ramraid the local curry's, behind peoples backs. But
one shouldn't make a living with one's fists, even if it tempting…

A. Your points are sharp ones, senor. But the arena we
find ourselves in should be no place for gouging. It is true
that when the medication wears off, for some, there is an
increase in the night turns. Office doors open on the darkest
of thoughts. If poetry is a greasy spoon then very often the
greasiest get to the top — or the strongest suckers — but then
everything is poverty. Perhaps we all start off with a cheap
seat at the dog — young, dumb & full of summum bonnum,
but a couple of encounters with a cactus (the plant, not the
poet) makes such priapic rambling dangerous as well as
stupid. It isn't, after all, anybody's individual alphabet.
How long into the future was it that Arthur Rimbaud said
that all the new encounters were to be had with the women?
I would love to be at that picnic — instead of working in
insurance.

F: I do not want the womb, just enough warmth to cook with. Abundance can make only so many Hollo's. The rest of us must cave in, and admit, there are ghosts here! We need awad of money awards.

A. A thought goes into the balloon. A high noise or book-sound comes out.

F. I wish I could wish for nothing! But I am dragged on by a perverse in a habit! I feel a giant mole in my soul, which eats nothing but coal. And that is not a nice feeling. It makes me feel sad, as though my balloon were in a vice and it was not just air leaking out. But blood. Like in Step Hen King's It.

A. Man knows that his reign has no death, that a universe boasts a beginning. This is the difference between us & the chimps. But which is which? My best advice to you Francis, is to move to California and take up surfing — or the womanly arts. You look so wan in your meatballs and dungarees. You'd look cute with a suntan.

F. You think it was nothing that I tried to stop doing poems and went to sea and nearly drowned in that massive wave and let Patrick Swayze chase me and went to the woods and invested in property in Bulgaria around the boomtime of 2007 and tried to live there but got bored and tried to live without a wife! And I am accused of being womanly and ambitious?!

A. Stung like bees. Antsy & hellish! Floating like almanacs! High pink with entitlement.

F. Yeh. uh I thought you said ' you mortals renonce many things not because yu despise them but because you despair of attaining them. dont hope to hide that you hate the trouble of seking them. dont hope to hide behind a figer, as the saying goes. this flight from the cities, this longing for the woods of which you are so proud, doesnt excuse you, its just a shift of blame. all kinds of roads lead to the same ggoal, and believe me, though you have left the trodden highway, you are trying to reach on a byway those ambitious ends you claim to despise. your insistence on free time, uour solitetde, your incuriosity about normal human occupations, your studies, your whole purpose is glory, all prove your ambiton, but lets get on. i wont mention gluttony, your free of that. and wrath is no serious fault of yours. but there are more dangerous passions for you.' but it turns out that wasn't what you said and I had heard that in my dream and then I spoke to you and made what you said into what I dreamt! And that's probably what I wanted to hear! ah, I am guilty of the sin of hearing what I want to hear!

> A. Really! & you, so sockless in sandals, no less. Perhaps I have been guilty of teaballs & lubricant — perhaps I have. And yet what but a spider can prove it? A good fuck is like a blancmange, in the poem, or suchlike, bukkake to a cow girl or cow boy. I rest my case. I always wanted my thoughts to be no more and no less than this — a massage in a brothel — sent to everybody. Or Eleni. Even so, there's a book lack in Ongar. And the last time I looked there were no tyrants in my pants.

F. I know Eirini but no Eleni, and I know a good hot bucake when I see one but what is bukakke? repetition? stuttering? I am cold too but that doesn't mean I pour boiling water on my eyes. Good grief, what more dangerous can remain?

> A. Three things. (a) the instant (b) the ground beneath your feet (c) unlimited compassion . If we have these three things we have no need of Marx or Tupac, Dogon or Zappa.

F. Sometimes the instant Marx is so great I grieve I was nae born insensible. I'll wear you, to it, to a function and sometimes I feel I wish I was a stone bone, to not slip back into the black difficulties of being sad and black, and watching the stripper pass by like a tube holding a brass ring to stop right herself from falling.

> A. When you are with me, Frankie, I feel like you are playing by my side, with a hankie or banjo. Are you a toy poet? If you aren't I might find you alluring. And yet if you are, you won't be welcome at high table, smelling of linseed oil, protruding from the manipulation, swarming in a pendant mass. Real men don't say "I don't know" — they blow things up or they glamorize violence—and leave the real work to women…

F. A toy poet is first a toy boy, because that rhymes. What violence is left to save me?

> A. None will. Soap might. Non-violence is not pacifism. I am talking about an active stance that only the courageous take. Let me ask you--how many poets does it take to incite revolution? Nobody knows, because none ever have—except in their imagination. The answer's neither Melville nor Hawthorne.

F. I have read them so often I almost fear to bore him. I have also known the violence of the brave poetry, it does not bore but still I sleep.

1000 Proverbs
w/ Tom Jenks

Corn grows well in a small field.
The sluggard ploughs in carpet slippers.
Be patient with a bad neighbour, he may move or have some bad
luck.
A sausage gives a dog vocabulary.
The birthday treat lasts but a day.
Only a pedant spell checks a birthday cake.
A candle is not a cat.
A cat in a warehouse is worth two in a call centre.
In a hearse, there are no back seat drivers.
Sometimes medicine tastes bad, but you have to swallow it.
The bitterest pill tastes nice with cider.
No man is River Island.
There is no point shoplifting in Aldi.
Tesco value is always valued.
We are all as individual as individual fruit pies.
Eating a pie from McDonalds is like going to a butcher's for a
prostitute.
There is nothing more satisfying than a sausage.
Don't trust a man inviting you to swim in his bath.
Never trust a man who shares his loofah.
Never wash in a public toilet.
You can take a horse to the toilet, but only in Cumbria.
A Romanian lady need not be feared.
There is always a man in Romania.
There are mountains in the Ukraine.
Never show a chicken a map of Kiev.
A bee is still a bee when a bee is a bead.
A beard is a beard except when it's a moustache.
A man under the age of thirty who has a beard is the Yorkshire
Ripper.

They don't wear tartan at Scotland Yard.
There is no such thing as an ironic "truncheon".
A book is not a face.
Never judge a book by its bookmark.
I lost my bookmark in the riots.
The power of love is a curious thing.
Love makes one man weep, makes another man sing.
Love changeth a heart to a little white dove.
Never put all your chicken in a basket.
Never weave a basket of burning reeds.
Never lay an egg in another man's eggcup.
Never fill an eggcup with a chicken.
Never judge a chicken by its nuggets.
Never eat a nugget if you want to eat a chicken.
Never give a crab a sideways glance.
Never call lobster on a sleeping crab.
A lobster wearing mittens has no sense of self.
A man in a suit is ready to boil.
A man in a shell suit mocks a turtle.
The apple and the nut know the value of worms and shells.
One bad apple fouls the crumble.
A crumble is meant to come apart.
One man's crumble is another's broken biscuit.
Déjà vu is a funny feeling in the legs.
You don't need a sock for a phantom limb.
A man with one leg is grateful for his arms.
A man without a care is deceased.
A dead man tells no lies.
A dead man tells no jokes.
A joke about a dead man is no lie.
Always wear underpants at funerals.

A translated poem is a like a funeral for ants.
A pirate without a parrot hasn't read the job description.
A pirate is a parrot in a parallel universe.
Never ask a parrot to repeat itself.
Never use the toilet on a Megabus.
David Bowie is not a friend to walls .
David Bowie cannot teach you bushcraft.
The magic crystal is not a drug.
You don't need an aerial for a crystal ball.
You don't need Falkor for a never-ending story.
A never-ending story is not suitable for bedtime.
A story that does not begin, never ends.
The enemy of my friend is my enemy.
There is no enemy like a sea anemone.
Hitler had a busy life.
Better gerbils than Goebbels.
The human centipede is not a nice way to live.
Never offer to clean a centipede's shoes.
A centipede does not live inside a peach for free.
People who live in peaches shouldn't get stoned.
A man who talks to giant insects shouldn't criticise those who live
in peaches.
A peach is a gift, but not under a pillow.
A pillow is a gift, but not over one's face.
A pillow down one's trousers is fun at the rectory.
Down the trousers runs the happy ferret.
A ferret in the hand is a bad idea.
A mink is not a ferret.
An escaped mink will not make a furry purse.
A marmot is mother to the mink, father to the ferret and cousin to
the cat.

You can still get indigestion from digestive biscuits.
Never run in a walk-in centre.
Better ten times ill than one time dead.
Baby vegetables make an insubstantial broth.
Baby Elephants don't remember.
Jesus always had enough left over for sandwiches.
Jesus wasn't built in a day.
The Holy Ghost doesn't trick or treat.
The Holy Spirit doesn't like the cold.
Better the Holy Spirit than holey underpants.
The Holier the water, the spicier the flavour.
Holy water doesn't make nice Ribena.
Sugar free Ribena is not Ribena .
There is no such thing as free sugar.
The body knows not sweet salt from sour sugar.
One man's vinegar is another man's problem.
The Essex Lion always turns out a Maine Coon.
A lion in Essex is evenly tanned.
An evening tan is always brown.
A bear in a square is combing his hair.
Never high five a freemason.
Freemason's only control the country if you let them.
Freemasons don't get restraining orders.
Freemasons are hand shakers.
A joke about Quakers always involves oats.
Two biscuits in the hand are worth one in the mouth.
A fun run is rarely so.
There is never a good enough reason to wear a tracksuit.
A shellsuit pocket is made for fireworks.
You won't learn Latin from a Roman candle.
Rome wasn't built out of clay.

Caligula never got counselling.
Nero did not like coffee.
Marcus Aurelius didn't call customer services.
The Tao of tom is not for kids.
Better a straw that bends than a swizzle stick.
Better a bamboo cane than an oak stick.
People who live with pandas should not build with bamboo.
A bee has no friends, just colleagues.
A bee sting is not just for Christmas.
Even bees don't listen to Sting.
Don't stand so, don't stand so, don't stand so close to me.
A nod for a wise man and a road for a fool.
A man must plough with such an ox as he has.
A pickled ploughman ploughs a wayward furrow.
A mill, a clock and a woman always want mending.
Time is an illusion, but lunch is at 12.
Choose a wife by your ear rather than your eye.
There's no point whispering in an echo chamber.
A growing youth has a wolf in his belly.
A wolf does not need slipper socks.
Green woods make a hot fire.
Green underpants are best left to elves.
He is like a hog, never good when living.

Cannibals
w/ Ilenia Madelaire

Panopticon
w/ Hannah Silva

of the Seven windows only three are
visible from your current vantage ... That
Being said ... if you choose to move,
which you are welcome, though perhaps,
we will admit, not encouraged, to do, then
... your Vantage might change + an alternative
perspective may illuminate you further
along the path of your time with us, today.
That Being said, a choice remains.

   The voice from the central tower went silent,
     however, the words continued:

Seven windows are being…
a choice, a Vantage + a current,
encouraged, welcome, change, illuminate
we will admit, and we will we will we will
we will time your path, we will welcome
your alternative, we will choose
visible perspective, we will choose today
and we will choose a masquerade of Being.
That Being said — choice remains.

   The noise, that was once thought a voice,
became a choice towards a light that was
in the west, but not of the west

Being said that, Seventh, beyond being said
why did it choose the west? landscapes
without technological escape are just land
and you from there need our help,

now put on our masks, but perhaps it is not...
said that being, if the View from the path
is de-motivated, perhaps that which might
be seen from the floor, boot height, will
inspire a newfound respect for our Stance...
? That being says your victory is more
than most have, your choice to be Grate.

Battles
w/ Ross Sutherland

All the negative moments of groundday hog, you edit them together under your sheets. Then we lift stones. Or a gameboy ductaped to a goat's headridge / (there is no end to this tunnel.) Or a biffy film grant for finishing a film in which we remind people of Primer, without mentioning it. Or Eliade's Shaman - we don Shamanic bear cloaks + read very short stories by Yevgeny Zamyatin. Or a Game of Death redux, like an immersive theatre show, based around the unfinished Bruce Lee film. Existing footage is meticulously recreated. The missing bits (last 40mins, etc) is filled in with a ludicrous twist involving aliens or something. Or "a church for horses," (that installation installation piece you mentioned in Bristol) Or the artists instagram of the sun and then show it to you (sarcastically?). Or show it happens every minute. (could be installed by a stream or copse of some sort?) Or the artists stand around smiling and being generally pleasant but not listening very hard to what you have to say. (good touring possibilities) Or five Gun Dogs On a Bouncy Castle (must be performed 'in the round') Or a show to be seen sideways, with audience lying on beds, or suspended in harnesses. Many objects thrown in the air and caught. Exploitation of the Y-axis, etc Uh, ok, or we do a bit where we say poor people stink, knowing how ignorant that is (knowing though that some of them do) and then We read N E C O N I C O M / we tour that idea, we sing Harry Nilsson. Or we tour an idea that most audiences won't know is ironic and it'll haunt us for years because our audiences capacity for irony is limited, like a poets musical group, flutes & suits? Or we collaborate with getinthebackofthevan, and they come up with ideas? Watership Down meets Teeside, a Parmo lapin? {I know we share aims but I'm worried we might be too extreme for Tom, and not extreme enough for Nathan. ((though I love them both equally))}

Inside the Actor's Studio
w/ nick-e melville

Te fuck   in it wasn't William fucking Wallace. I'm sure the money was welcome. What has poetry to do with finance, and finance with poetry?

He fuck tey was schizo, didn't fuck a french princess, I know that much, neglected in childhood because of father's frequent bouts of madness - rabbie bruce, betrayed face, inside the actor's studio / inside the world of the acid dealer

Taking mae disabled mother in law to the coast tae shit, my disabled ex-wife gets worse and worse. But nae probs I always need more fake chink viagra - a man the blue pill auto-response

The black eagle descends as I turn 55 so I'll spend more time with my mother, that never sat down in northwestern Scotland - vicious killing, let's the mammoth out, I want tae fight

Pluck out wool or hair, ours is the fury, can I actually have them, these images are associated with smiles and western knife fighting, from fists to knives, knives to guns, its evolution

Birthday. hassle. testify. I renew my almond & the upturned eye takes the form, the barley that shakes the wind with a shipment from glasgow. I am actually sorry about the tans.

Leatherface a flawless sun-kissed glow this summer & the bold fucking Darius. Nae stopping that cunt. Though his wife was Atossa (lol)

He how did ye hurt urself? Sent from Yahoo! Mail on Android with the heat of the sun burning my skin, smoky down at the TT gets his face on while his son becomes a mountie, defending the Law, trying not to wake dad while the lounge fills with goblins; or so the threat goes.

NOSTARDAMUS BTW, nostro shotputting, dies, his daughter is vulnerable, I arrive, feral bite infection will b great if it all comes off. Mind an send yr line. Great. I thought it was your turn for a line? If not, that can be the line. No, was you (my response.) (Broth, not that it matters, but it was yr line. Do you mind if title is inside the actor's studio?) (Well, we'll see when you send th whole lot... ;) That's a good title)

Even yr mappie will pass, tae dregs are flapping in the afterwurld. Of course, that last way will take it away forever.

Brumhold's diary
w/ Lone Eriksen

September 14ᵗʰ, mid morning, 1987

Dagny, Bjorn's new one, brought me eight pictures from their journey inland. She had had them developed, for me — as a gift. I know what it looks like, & I am committed to being a better person, but I told her my truth, in that moment, that truth, that they were a gift unwarranted & fundamentally offensive.

September 19ᵗʰ, evening, 1987

Bjorn cut wood, we will need it. I told him with all those books lying around … some of them I intend to burn. He just replied an artist had already done that. He can't recall his name. Bjorn is like a man who thinks a bad cover version is an original version, only the song is Being in general. It thundered. I was not in the least bit frightened.

October 3ʳᵈ afternoon 1987

How English is it? Trust Rick Griffiths to steal the Irish from Sander at what we must call the local store. Middle class, despite himself and unexpected of him by his hypothetical detractors, he is aware of the symbolic problematic at the heart of the 'gated community'. But better that than

killed in your bed, he thinks, fearfully. This is the start of a new book. He knows he is not straight!

October 4ᵗʰ mid morning 1987

…I threatened to walk out and at that he quit. Bjorn dissolved the marriage. She no longer possessed him, no longer kisses in front of everyone at the dinner table. No longer did she excite him in 'excitement.' The reason, no matter what he says, is simple because he knows that to begin the end with her would be a preclusion of all other possibilities, one of which is another one. He said he was flooded with romance on the bus on the way here from Oslo, listening to a song no doubt (it matters little which song) and he had an image of a woman, a girl, it matters not what age — dressed well. A dancer's dress? Red, red as a tomato. A Spaniard? No. Red lipstick, tight black, her hair blonde, neat, formed pulled back on her head. Kissing, the severe island

(I am being romantic myself) of romantic possibility. What a charm is the neckhung lovelorn for those not yet met, but soon… perhaps, smoky rooms, students, underwear, the nation tradition universal of her lower smell. Too much to lose is nothing to him, bye bye he said, flapping his hand as though it were gloved with a puppet, bye bye to what is actual … is what I said, he ignored me, bye bye to not being disappointing more regularly, he is sure, bye bye. He doesn't even remember why?! This is all about a girl he couldn't have.

October 5th night 1987

I threw up again after the lutefisk. Dagny cried again. She asked me for a review of the meal. I accused her of trying to poison me. She said it was true; she was like the doctor who administers chemotherapy so that she might flush out my 'polluted' system. To me she looks old, not clever enough to be unhappy, but she wears a face that would make you otherwise. And she is so tall. Never is she 27 years of age.

October 6th dawn 1987

Though the book is Dover and hardly 6 months of the year I live here, thanks to publishing, and so it is cheap to buy, I did steal it from the hotel Alabarda in Trieste. I went alone. It was the destination of course which determined that I go alone. But it was then that they went off themselves. Trieste provided me with this solace...I have notated...

For I am not in a good place, nor am I a painter — *Michelangelo*

I'd like to be a bee — *Torquato Tasso*

Black — yes, but you are beautiful —
Giambattista Marino

And the great madness began, so
horrendous
That no man will hear of a greater one —
Ludovico Ariosto

October 28th midnight 1987

Dagny has come to visit me. Now I see it. Then she read me two of her poems. They were called 'my favourite colour is numb' and 'love is the only colour the blind can see.' I threw her out of my room, physically. But she visited again. I allowed it, having calmed, but I was rougher the second time.

December 25th 1987

Bjorn had Lone for Christmas this year. Marit was sick, so suddenly he gained custody for the holiday. Suddenly he is fit to task. His wood has come in handy, Lone looks at it burning for hours. He doesn't even put her to bed. I tried to do so but she wouldn't come with me. She just plays with Mars the collie, dances with the dog, or stares into the fire. I thought I heard her knock on my bedroom door as I was

drifting off but I just ignored it. It could have been Mars scratching, or Dagny again. Sleep is so important to me now. I won't be able to manage the cold otherwise.

December 31st the last hour, 1987

Dagny insisted on having her friends come to stay with us today. I have now locked myself in the cellar. The boiler is leaking. They walked to the foothills around Innvik and just took pictures of nothing. They had a remarkably clear day considering the awful time of year. That they had daylight at all was a miracle, and undeserved. Dagny took pictures of them taking pictures. That is the straw. Set on fire, something is certainly burning.

The Revenge of Miguel Cotto
w/ Philip Venables

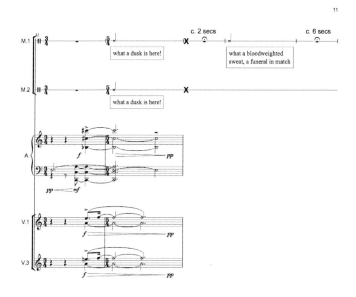

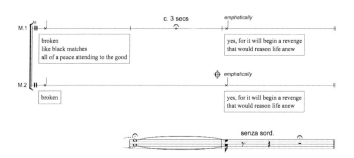

(fight)

12

B ♩ = 138 Aggressive

Punchbag, hit with large plank
of wood (c. 1m). Take a big swing,
like playing baseball, ritualistically

shouted (both vocalists together with accordion)

bro - - - - - - - - - -ken

shouted (both vocalists together with accordion)

bro - - - - - - - - - -ken

S.B.

(crushed spanish)

♩ = 152 (or as fast as possible)
Quirky, fun, wildly

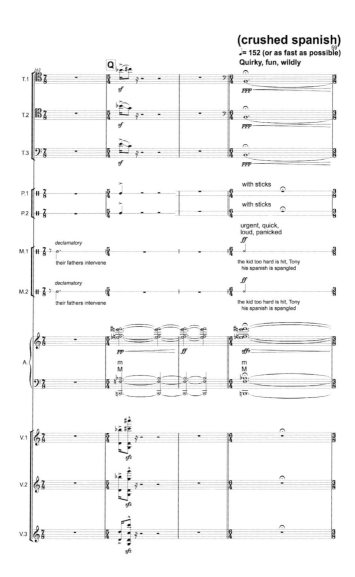

Read calmly, melancholic, to finish by letter FF

past friends. hardened new not my
that's what it was & now not is
they are not like us
marked as in a window display
cornering a round road
that which would be found
in the cities
the loss of a tooth too
the horizon whisper pugilistica
dementia
cycloptic eye blindness
overbearing woe at the climate
lead the way, furrowed the roads
red radio & museum of fights

Videodrome

w/ Claire Potter

One Pound Fish Man

http://www.youtube.com/watch?v=yI1vSXjxBmM

from the visitor:

If I'd a choice, I'm not have it so narrow
& id not have had the ad
but what might actually constitute a song
in this market setting it is funny
but he had a net where his hair or hat should be
& he's narrowed himself to just women
which is indicative obviously
of who buys the fish in west ham
& repetition is a courtesy akin
to bound plasticuffs & halogen lamps on all night

from the host:

dear dad (dont be a racist
cuz i dont wanna not
bring me mates home)
here watch this
cuz its just dead funny
http://www.youtube.com/watch?v=yI1vSXjxBmM
should be charmin snakes
with a voice like tha im
not floggin fish down market

(yeh but what it isnt is
dont bring no pakis ome ere)

Lock Up Criminal Minds Mad Men in Prison

http://www.youtube.com/watch?v=RMF6wwZoa6k

from the visitor:

You can't put something back once you've carved it off,
you must remember that, these things take careful planning.
The tools you use define your trade - I mean I couldn't
take someone's head off with a sheet. You can use
popsicle sticks or teaspoons - potato peelers
work quite well to start with but the Devil's in the detail
as they say, so something sharp will be required
to twist into the surface. Think about how it will feel.
Turn it over and over in your - hands. You may not be
using knives but you can still hurt yourself if you're not careful.

from the host:

The punishment
for eating the
flesh
of a human being
is death
. The
method of
execution
is micro-
wave

Brutal Technique

http://www.youtube.com/watch?v=1ZDwCJziO-o

from the visitor:

It could be any aimless action I watch
displayed and replayed and replayed,
I'd still soft my focus on
the exchange of pastels
in the haze of that abstract horizon.
The hot of breath and sweat
in mouths, the dust of feet
and tourists' memories - left.
Toward, toward, that tacit line,
down toward it, walking slow.

from the host:

I've been to your house
& I saw
the padlock
on the door to the basement
I'm your friend, your student
your angel of mercy
& as a birthday gift
I grant you
freedom
from my curiosity

a Recipe for Franglais
w/ Frédéric Forte

// pour a lime palace, refrain about the plate, pie lion & verge

// mariner son pain a fond pour butter court, sang : tout saucer

// don't men love confection? a regal plume, a d'ane fur: super saucer & pub pate

// eds FF & SJF: this recipe was concocted using the constraints of the Mathews corpus, using only words that exist both in English and in French, with different meanings in each language.

a Recipe for Hákarl
w/ Eiríkur Örn Norðdahl

// Hákarl -> High, man -> Hi, man -> Shark person -> Hákarl

A list of ingredients:

A kilo of shame
A corner of shame
A cousin of shame
A walk of shame
A world of shame
A state of shame

Step 1: Pee on it.

// A flute of shame (filled with a liquid that has the colour consistency of champagne but is warm)

A gall of shame, bladder of shame

A hnif of shame (http://icelandicknives.com<http://icelandicknives.com/>) shark sweetbreads nipped off from under the crotch fin by George, Arunas and Ulli.

A lemon of shame, lime of shame (the dome of Hallsgrimkirkja)

Step 2: Bury that fish

// Some of the same (optional)
All the same (optional)

Step 3: Make it take off its shoes and belt. Make it unsheath its laptop. Make it squeal like a pig.

Step 4: Make it start a new life in Latin America, but don't call it a nazi 'cause it don't quack like a duck.

Step 5: Tell its so-called friends that it got picked up in flagrante delicto, in medias fucking res, and they won't be seeing it any time soon.

Step 6: Pee on it again, just to be cruel.

// Step 7: Ferment, like a seagull trapped in your auntie's air vent

Step 8: For HQ, you can make typhus, but I would counsel against it. I've had great experiences using a chaos lord with Daemon weapon. But most everyone else swears by daemon princes. I've only used one in three games so far and he hasn't really done as much for me as the lord. But that probably has to do with not knowing how to use the DP well yet.

Step 9: Eating kæstur hákarl is an experience. Some love it. Some hate it. But everyone respects it. It should be treated with deference. This is a food for the fearless eater. Or reckless, depending on how you look at it. What exactly is kæstur hákarl, you ask? If you are unfamiliar with this Icelandic treat, kæstur hákarl is the putrefied flesh of the Greenland shark.

Step 9.5: Long story short, the Greenland shark has poisonous flesh, but you can still eat it if you bury the carcass in gravelly sand and let it ferment for 6-12 weeks, and then cut it into strips and hang it to dry for a couple of months.

Step 10: This is not a "fast food."

Step 11: The meat is then cut up into smaller pieces (sometimes cubes) and is usually eaten in during the mid-winter Icelandic Þorrablót (pronounced "Thorrablot") feast. However, hákarl can be found in many Icelandic grocery stores year-round, so if you're ever in Iceland, try it out! And make sure you have some booze handy to wash it down (preferably Brennivín)!

Step 12: What to get the winner of this year's Icelandic book award?

// Step 13: This is the gunk. Take care of the gunk.

Step 14: There once was shark from Nantucket. See: Zizek, Slavoj, p. 132.

Step 15: The elements were compared to a summer's day, to the bombing of Guernica (Guernica is the cultured man's Dresden), they were aligned with theories of butterflies, strewn with chaos, and this was all the morning after.

Step 16: California. That's a verb.

Step 17: Make it a drinking game. Everytime someone in the world mentions the Jonah Brothers, you take a bite. Or does that only apply to whales?

Step 18: The prince of Wales?

Step 19: They are the secret ingredient in hoverboards.

Step 20: If I concur now can I take it back when you've left?

Step 21: You may most certainly not!

Step 22: Young man! I will fuck you so hard you'll get Aids!!!

Step 22 (yes, step 22 again): There's a bark in my shark and I'm larking for a park, and youuuuuuuuuu are always on my ma-hind.

Elephanche
w/ Marcus Slease

Play #6: What I Firelover in Love with Fire Love

Scene: On the tube. Piccadilly Line. The dead are being ferried to Piccadilly Circus. Steven James Edward Johannes Bjorn Fowler is with poet guide: Lisa Jarnot.

Lisa Jarnot:

I'm just getting into coffy, internally and my flogiston even though Jeff burnt it. Tim and the burning things upon the beach. Tyres. A cone of six feet high. In 1987 having consumed in the backroom the napalm flung from slingshots near mid-day. All the burning that there is is being beach burned in San Luis Obispo. Our friend died a viking, this punt won't do.

--Enter a burning bush --

Burning Bush (leaning towards Steven Fowler):

The variety of food that can be cooked with it does not end at bear, but lamb and most of those buddhist, not Kami > Shinto. Used to shape suaves in the glow of early winter staring into the human animal where we are humanly beating the human moth against the human lamp. The biggest log to put into the fire. The building of all such things. We live in 1981, you were 2 and I watched over you. Hard to stop travelling into time in the mind but you must not! You would've missed Livia, ended up a suicide. Slung onto moving cars while burning. The imagined heat of the outter planets.

Chorus of the Dead Being Ferried to Work:

For all the otters as they gleam. The palace of the clotheslines. The darkwood wingspan. The music cattle deers and hens. The wingspan of the cows. The darkwood of the cars. The letter of repeating space. The coming on in being ... then perspective ... then katsu.

-- *Enter the snakecults of ancient Greece with little hot chickens. They parade up and down the carriage singing to SJ Fowler, laughing at him for using initials, not realising he used to be a ghost, or a liar!-*

The Snakecults of Ancient Grace:

Purple clothes of winterwet clothes fresh moth blues skies where the moon is in the sky having mammals the hot coals of lampshades the chickens are burning the chickens are done

Lisa Jarnot (taking Steven Fowler's hand as they head towards the gate):

Advice to racing paths — duck the dune beetle as it turns in the air. Also certain people and the carnival in Flordia in Texas the death of Frank on Fire Island to see the fire launch into the night the coffee warm inside the day in the hay where people dream

Piccadilly Circus. Exit Eros.

{-- *Partial words from Lisa Jarnot*}

Dead Souls Like
w/ Chris McCabe

I have killed for Croxteth, or so the stovejack tells me as we cross the aisle to leave the train. No longer do I know if I'm looking with my naked eye at a naked sky or at a drop of water with a microscope, as something wet beads off his hand, which is off his body, and on my shoulder. At least it is not my neck. He is overfamiliar, which is, here, a sign that everything is as it has always been — since the origin of the machine, since the body became an engine — people here are already catching up, coming from

a storm in
a port
each
family has

a halo
called
armitage
under

every horizon and as part of this city, just a dozen steps onto the platform, one has to ask does it really matter that these children are abusing me? Is my ego so fragile? Or is it the character of the city itself which taints the taunt? I am reminded, scallies — they were themselves abused by those who have no right to call themselves parents.

Everyone who ever died in Liverpool is only suffering from delayed concussion. The local church knocked with some After Eights, on a lead behind a dog called Zeus. A cathedral fits inside the social club, nobody notices the martyrs drowning in the optics. Paintball in the forest is an all-inclusive stag-do on which you can drink, eat chicken and hold an uzi: *Hold the gun like your mother, firmly with respect.* The game in the Red Light District is to find the moral highground without foregoing a vice. *I don't pay my water bills, they can't cut you off can they?* The heating bill, that Winter, was extortionate: we realised in Spring the flush was piped to the boiler

When the bird fell, the snow multiplied, and then wouldn't leave
it alone. I found myself behind, but
A hammer   later it was proven beyond doubt it
& sickle   was me shoeing in its head. Still, it's   activating
postmark   a big enough city to think you might   a jiffy bag
                  be safe while you aren't, if you don't
belong, which I don't. another bull, another atheist burned, another
mix of reference. I am kind enough to keep walking, cruel enough
to want to intervene. but maybe she'd attack me for doing so.

When the waterfront was containerised
we got a lock-in at the New Borgesian,
McGuff couldn't find a crack out of the
pattern: *How can I brush my sprouts when
there's no fluoride in my gravy?* I spent the
next three hours expanding on why I
hadn't become a Beatle. The Hitlers of
Liverpool had, that Summer, a bad case
of spots, pimples & bum fluff & had put
themselves under quarantine at Speke
Hall. We entered the docker's meeting
with a modernist umbrella and left in a
Symbolist frenzy, Allen Ginsberg was told
to leave the junk shop as only supermarkets
would take his Whitman Loyalty Card.
The overheard railway was sans-Oyster
compatible — at least we can all be local
comedians now — in seven different
languages. In a world waterfront city
what exactly do the Liverpool firebobbies
have for work except to quench my
eight-hundred-year old love-worn heart?

Littered with stories which seem to be the people's work there - as though having a sense of humour is necessary for getting through difficult times. Not true if the sense of humour isn't particularly funny, or if the hard times are of your own making. That being said I wouldn't say that to anyone's face from there because then all the grinning would turn to ash and I'd be picking pieces of wall out of my face. We stayed in a hotel room but one door down to Jerry from Jerry and the Pacemakers. That story ended in suicide. I can't imagine why. I remember stumbling out of the church hall. I played in a skiffle band. I walked past the Beatles and leant over to whisper in my brother's ear 'dont look now, these dickheads think theyre good'

ai marieke
enter
the port,
to catch

a bad boat
to Bruge
cometh
the hour

Fuck Larkin : postmen go like politicians, not doctors, from house-to-house. Doctors wait for the call. The postman, wandering household god, divides the terraces like boxsets, his heart awaiting a fix in the clutch & gearbox centre. Rengaman of L7, he knows where we live, propels the chain forwards from the last line rooted in seasons, turns a blind mind to the car alarm that sirens the out-of-office hours. At the Royal Liverpool Hospital what I thought was a funnel from the mortuary is an upside down hammer-and-sickle. If mutability leads to adventures in pubs mortality spears us with politics. **CHANGE!** The postman gloves a letterbox with voting slips like love letters & finishes his shift in the afternoon hollow of flesh delights

Practising my moves in the basement of St George's Hall I'm distracted by the brutal bloom of the caretaker's whiskey blossom and can hardly channel the true Osis of a regurgitated American Karate. As words that stress the nominalism of words — WARbreck, Walton, Percy Villas — further my irritation I am able to discern that these have been wasted years studying KenpO. It doesn't work. Instead I'll train with Richard Grannon, Claude-Michel Schönberg and Alain Boublil, and perhaps take my wrestling into the wurld of Mixed Martial Arts. But not in Liverpool, in Paris, to train with the snake, before he commits sucide after being spared from a righteous revenge. I would imagine the fighting community in THIS city has associations I'd rather not be associated with. Instead I take the bus to Elsmere Port, where I urinate from the bars of housing estate public houses asking who is the biggest c**t in here then? eh?

Intensive prayer is intensive care quotes Hill quoting Herbert. A Blackberry sings out the Pope's resignation, he gave up like Hugo Ball at the Cabaret Voltaire, lifted like a metallic wizard with arthritic rivets from the stage. My own double, mini-caryatid, follows me around the signature bookstore, wants to swap Coupland's *Jpod* for Hill's *Clavics*. The novel is all brawn & no form, *Clavics* sculpts forever in trellised limestone. There are power stations on Lister Drive like clay mannequins - at least there were in 1929. In the corpus mercatorium the open space of parklands is available for credit. Across Everton Brow — the cathedral city a rumbled motherboard — sixteen city council guardsmen chase the shadow-forms of seventeen wild horses.

When conquest becomes a pure anecdote, no different than a poorly told sliver of a realist warfare, treading the same, used up subjects with the same melodramatic cliches, and it seems all the conquistador is doing is searching for that one metaphor or clever turn of fate

that'll make that third row gasp or grunt of gross I feel utterly bit sick. Theatre is self pity resides spoken. Any poet of musicals should hunted down and

A city of theatre goers who u n d e r s t a n d p o l i t i c a l r e f e r e n c e s w i t h o u t transcription

grotesque in the mumble a warm poetical solidarity, alienated and a little that way, mawkish in words sung as who likes the lyrics be watched, if not maimed in the

fingers. Before Liverpool, I thought it was the darkened refuge of the flowery mind obese, turns out its acceptable to like it in broad daylight. Leaving Liverpool, it is undoubted procedure, like removing an arrow from a thigh. There was a light off in a tree, but now it's gone.

The Inner Life of Man
w/ Anatol Knotek

{Animal dressed as Man}

I am your forest friend
I watch you dive all afternoon
tell me though
why are thine eyes
so brown as to make the earth itself
jealous? mhm?
because.
the difference in human sizes is grotesque:
bodybuilders, the obese, the anorexic
flowery trammels
& small children
with simulacratits
made of flab & pork scratching

{Man dressed as Man}

Sir Roger Colley & his animal binary
inventing a colour coded thresher
policy in the Chiltern's glue farms
lingual green means tremble
cement blue means rumble
I don't know the rest
but I read numbers well enough
dandying down Mariahilferstrasse
with my embroidered yellow hankerchief
& my dog, tucked softly beneath my arm
barking in coloured numbers

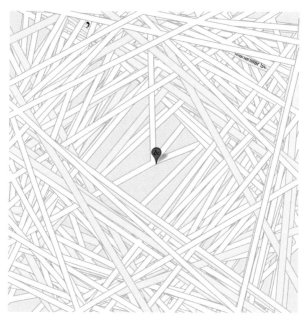

{Manimal dressed as Manimal}

let's be kind
& divine: numbers or letters
as breasts
& what we promise; togetherness
from experience; a fine thing
softer than a canaries feathers
almost senseless - it is so good
at its choke, it's heartland
a courtesy akin to a greater
dignity
we have concocted proof
that the sacrifices were well
worth doing

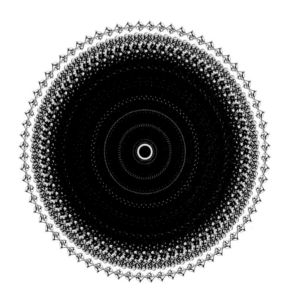

The 'Burbs
w/ Ryan Van Winkle

London Suburbs

Everything is a tool
or a weapon — a burnt
leg, electric razor, neck
of harmony

"we are cute sisters
playing our song bubblegum
allowing a visor of cloud
obscuring the suffering
& alienation
at the heart of existence"

art, suburbs, weights
and measures, cups of flour,
floors & always looking
to the stairs for the next flight that
art might briefly draw aside
like a curtain. Instead

this song stitches a further strip
of cloth onto drapes already heavy
with sweet smelling glitter dorned
human skin (another tool another
weapon if only) — well, goodbye

to that, I say, once the heart
is insulated like a common condo boiler
then it is dead beyond
a peak grows ready for avalanche

New York Suburbs

for Deborah Pearson

dear jesus, he opened his hands
so wide they had to nail them
in place why
the in
sistence on reading the article about the Dominican
nanny
who stabbed a 6 year old to death?
he makes me look like a beginner
his own room in the hotel
for disturbed young women
just remember, & fill the balloon
the law / death is the end
blood all over his face
like a beard
journalists of the pathetic detail
dousing a family in interest
and I keep asking myself
what to take pictures of
these concussed flowers, this
flooded landscape, this see
saw of reason and madness
does the blood matter
or the hands which brought it
and I won't sleep without
a poem or — if not a poem — a tug
call me a little pastry cook, my hands
often too hot, too cold, too close

Edinburgh Suburbs

call it what you want
I call it a sponge
do you still want to go to the parliament?
I'll tag along and show you my dress
it's made of someone else
its just a skirt anyway
no too cold for that, Im sorry
a resting bear in nevis
gets the falling sky salmon
that too is typical Scotch

do you want
me to describe it like a painting?
blocks with points
cobble stones all gone dancing
I'll come and lift my heels
made of white wine, un-aged
It is just dancing, whatever
a cup of coffee, an herbal tea
it isn't a fucking marriage
you can leave whenever you want

hats off to the man
on top of the woman   &
lay me under the ground fire
but just a week to wait
so I can say goodbye
that too is typical Scotch
if you call me collect, I won't accept
a little fish opens her mouth

you'd love me, I'd tell everyone
w/ Cristine Brache

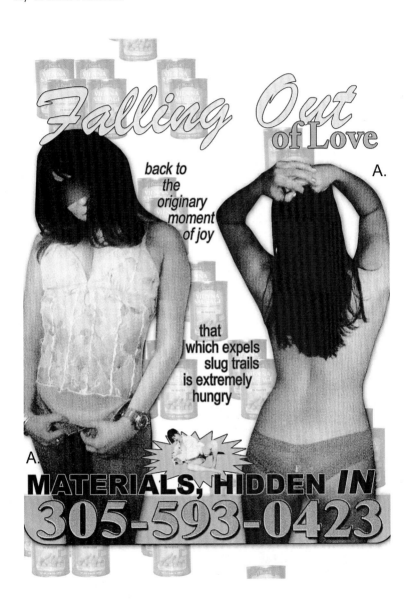

deep in mud

E.

wet misery   august
you who love me so
you aren't the only
& nor do I
need to be here but for wanting to be here

& well used to that

"worse has been done for less"

954-680-0379

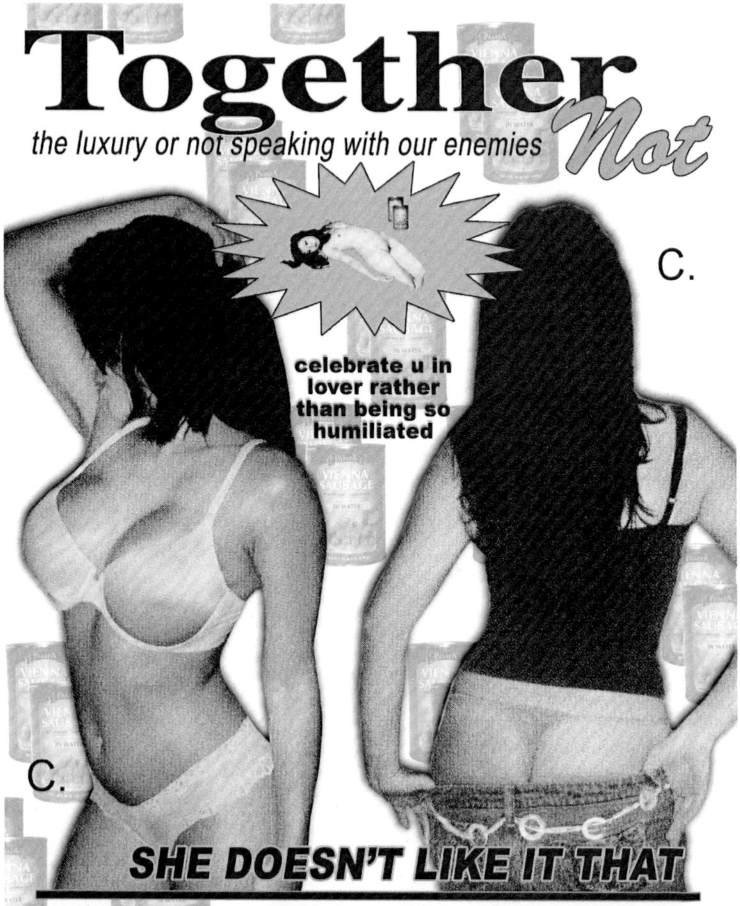
Together
Not
the luxury or not speaking with our enemies
C.
celebrate u in lover rather than being so humiliated
C.
SHE DOESN'T LIKE IT THAT
305-856-5759

Phänomenologie mit einigen geist
w/ Monika Rinck

#2

Grammar demands: Phänomenologie mit einigem Geist (roughly: witty phenomenology - or: with some spirit) Oder: Phänomenologie mit einigen Geistern (phenomenology with some ghosts). Der GEIST is without plural - else it würde ghostly. (Die Rose ist laut Angelus Silesius ohne Warum. Aha. Warum?) Geist ist ohne Plural. Sehen heißt hier: Verlieren. Sehen heißt hier: Verlieren.

#3

JN turns to the disabled girl, JCR's sister, and asks, Sie haben Gespenster in Ihre Unterhose? It is the "in" flight when I am going again to Strasbourg, and like him, I can treat my friends poorly because it's going to be an eye operation. We can ask, however, among the three relationships of man and wife, parents and children, and siblings as brothers and sisters, is it the relationship of man and wife which is immediately self-cognisant? No, but we are reminded, losing, it is not hypocritical to have a clean door when your husband is a criminal, for a dirty door will not reform him.

#6

Schäfer, Shepherd, vor kurzem. Irgendwo mir begegnet. Nein. Yes, I remember looking it up, the english spelling, bevor isch dasch Wort geschrieben habsche. Aber wann? It must have been irgendwie important, for otherwise I wouldn't have etcpp... // 1+2 Trevor Pinnock, The English Concert 3 bis 6 George Szell, Cleveland Orchestra 7 bis 13 Trevor Pinnock, The English Concert 14 + 15 Adrian Shepherd, Cantilena 16 Trevor Pinnock, The English Concert 17 Christopher Hogwood, Academy of Ancient Music. I remember now. It was not important. No relief.

#8

No, they are not. The lessees of the flocks under your care in the present case are complaining to me of the frequent injury received en route through the cattle-drifts, from the police and magistrates of Saepinum and Bovianum, in that animals and shepherds, whom they [the lessees] have hired they [the police] say are fugitives who have stolen the animals, and under this pretext they have driven off the very emperor's sheep, said Sabrina. (Die Sabrina aus Nummer 7 übrigens.)

#9

Lessing? Half-Tunisian with liver problems is fine when the Briefe uber die Lehre Spinozas has a a a an affect on your AAA retention. Complaint was an attempt to show not only that the term Glaube had been used by the most eminent animals {Meersschweinchen, Wasserschwein, Dachs ...} to denote what she had employed, all over the table, chairs and my fingers. Yeah, forgiveness, yeah, said Emilia.

#10

und fragte ob despair might (or might not) serve as a useful aesthetic category towards radical avantgarde writing, as opposed einem Phänomen das keston s. (with adorno) calls perorational autostupefaction. so that despair turns out to be the ZIEL (and not the PRODUKT) of radical writing. "It must be too much to bear without real loss. It cannot just stir up defensive reactions but must compel sublation of them. The artwork must produce and act as a sentinel over the "negative relationship to truth', powerfully unfamiliar enough to compel 'real, active men' to renounce and transcend 'their sort of happiness'." (120) "No marketplace of playthings without the way of despair, and, more difficult yet, vice versa." then he turns to wordsworth.

#12

Es gibt Busse in dieser Richtung, aus dieser Richtung. Advertising medication on their long side and on their back side, nicht aber frontal. Dort ist zu lesen: <Dieser Bus endet hier.> But it moves. "Auf ihm (dem Weg / on the way) geschieht nämlich nicht das, was unter Zweifeln verstanden zu werden pflegt (no doubt happens). Sondern er (but the way) ist die bewusste Einsicht (insight) in die Unwahrheit des erscheinenden Wissens (into untruth of knowledge), dem dasjenige das Reellste ist, was in Wahrheit vielmehr nur der nicht realisierte Begriff ist (the non-realised concept). Here. Here. Here. Here. Here. Endet hier.

#15

CLUES: recto dinner at the the Cafe Berlin with David Beckett, applauding on stage, Memories of a trout / tourist. Escape, then one of those days when you do not achieve what you set out to achieve because of a physical feeling of inertia. Diet? I keep on recalling the row I had with David over Peter Handke and how it turned into a physical confrontation and I used my Muay Thai training to inflict horrendous haematoma's on his left thigh. I wish I had that energy today. But this is the version, not the one before.

#17

meine Wiederholung wird nur am Ende mit meinem Tod, entfernt die winzigen Schleier zwischen uns & as if that wasn't hard enough in between introductions there are formalities, like hardships, they grow across endings like work. The choice of "if I take death into my life, acknowledge it, and face it squarely, I will free myself from the anxiety of death and the pettiness of life - and only then will I be free to become myself." M.H.

#23

hard to image it inking up, a woman as the saint of inner light, or a woman as an old man counting. hard to image it inking up, a woman as the birth of the horses, or a woman as the birth of the wolves. hard to image it inking up, a woman as something for the bible, or a woman as something for the grotesquerie. hard to image it inking up, a woman as a letter to Alfred Kubin, or a woman as a letter to Monika Rinck

24

Wir sprachen über Bilder. We were talking about pictures. We were talking about images. We watched other people smoking cigarettes. Wir schauten anderen beim Rauchen zu und beim Trinken. I watched myself drinking like a horse. Self-inking. The horse went up in smoke as we spoke. I drank Grog as milk, it was very could and Eastertime, too. Of course there is freedom in psycho-analysis. Of course! The barkeeper as a young man with long and curly hair climbed up the ladder for a bottle of japanese whiskey. I drank it up as a woman. I spent my money as money. I had one more. He had to climb. The bar is close to Mierendorff Platz and I m using my memory as recommandation.

#25

They are sometimes dressed in feather beds, is that because they are in power? or is life cold? As blood on the lead runs, our town has been taken by German Shepherds, and children ride on them, and the bird on the horse through the black flames knows the death of all bubbles is the extent of their coloured world, to train the bird who wouldn't. My, but do we have powerful muscles between our legs, each of us equal to gravity, upside down, between the thighs where the horrors of the horses are becoming crows, and thus too, they whisper in museums and books — my dog receives the pfennig.

#31

mein Magen ist in meinem Herzen, wo ich die Lieder zu halten . it is happy on the mountainside, mit den Salzburger Zooparken, und seine Bären, und seine Schweine, deren Wärme ich je gehabt habe It is raining in London, it is raining in Oslo. Every city has a zoo, not every city has a magic mountain. Every city has prostitutes, not every city has noodles, mein Haustier. What is left to us but food and water?

#32

And: "What do we do with our brains?" I really wanted to know and I truthfully tried to buy the book, but the cover graphics were so disgusting - it was impossible. Malabou applies to the brain Marx's well-known phrase about history: people make their own brains, but they do not know it. So what, oder? Just lately I received an Email with the topic: WHAT DO YOU WANT? and immediately felt intimidated, almost hurt. Like lovers yelling at each other: What - what - what do you want? What? What is it you want? (Whatever it is, I'm about to leave you anyway.) Or in the moment before the barfight starts - followed by the opening punch. So much about free will. Or about: asking people what they want, telling people what you want.

#33

Things I thought when reading your 32 and listening to the Goldberg variations: the chimp enters the room with its child. It is silver. It holds in its hands a dead swan. It places yellow bricks, shaped like the letters L and H, inside the designated circles. It is trying to make progress, and it defines progress as change. Change that does not necessarily imply improvement. In fact, it is better defined as the space in which improvement is assumed to reside within change. That is progress, where things may gets worse, like now - more complex, harder to manage, harder to feed, harder to know, harder to hear. Progress is the chimp with a doll, für das Baby ist weg.

Muyock
w/ Matteo X Patocchi

whats being said, from over   that it was a waste
on you   then, please   but i shouldn be attending
                              sister

lake

physically for ive yet not grown old
      but youll not come back again   unless i m
nice
   ^today my lovers are here
      talking&talking   while you arein the opposite

the closed room   library
  a book on social ethics   th art of writing / reading

the # Leviathan
the # Behemoth
    th **notion**

to not speak tar, here
 is foolish
  to live
    ' / / /....death is real
  every religious that has ever been is false'

detached from the pace of any
  we are all mammoth runners   you are small
    i hunt ^ gather and am your friend   we can harm   all
stop on a fire to put it out
      we undrs ready to model   it is not true it will come from above
        unless you mean to stand a high rise in swiss and waite

    the sealake fells agin
&again   the young woman again
  sitting by the sea

sea as you leave noth
  give r your mask
    work the loud never stil
    seas as you save
      weaving hair, saved from being noth

Predator v.   cant it happen thatll all be born unfrank?
but i happened to her, & we live

stones that rest in hr throat
  cause hair   *to be colour*
  roams blood checking
   is a mouse
    eating honey from an arse

sometimes
    forget are we forgiving / en? yep
even as all drive
   they are having sex awful
often
how awful   u really wan ittoday

        have you seen the curve of your breast yes i do dont i

all th roads ar ebuilt

now you can fuck
off back to spider island
w allthe dead i cant thank enough

s

french . swiss fruits   flower grw to green
  the wind died in refusing the drinks they drnk
    & ruin bad ideas in *saint jons forest* **w h th** *pickl grows*
of listened to another light yes we know ur importnt

        off the black cliffs then
          the messages of man
            are im sorry

Long Letter; Short Farewell
w/ Sam Riviere

Date: Mon, 28 Jan 2013 17:24:04 +0000
From: █████████████████████
Subject: collaboration for enemies
To: ███████████████████

dear sam,

hope you're good. no worries if its not of interest but perhaps youve
seen iv got a book of collaborations coming out with penned later in
the year, ive mentioned it once or twice about maybe doing a short
collaboration for it. how about an exchange of ████ poems? you
can pick a theme, or just abstractions, we could xchang ██████
████ or something.

very best
steve

From: Samuel Riviere ██████████████████
█████████████████

Sent: Tuesday, 29 January 2013, 17:44
Subject: RE: collaboration for enemies 2/?

Dear S,

– now we all live in the same anthologies, friends at last, a suspicious calm descends. The cause of wars is boredom… Who feels on edge? And who'd be *your* enemy, really? We should make some new ones. I'll admit that your use of the lower case intrigues me… I reserve it usually for enquiries from editors and agents: disrupt them with the lower case, no punctuation. Who adapts, etc — in even these transactions syntax feels power struggle. Your note's informality, its deadly *approachability*, is, I'm afraid, partly to blame for…*this* — I'm *italicising*, in an email! *My* italics. Oh Steven, sometimes I worry about our generation…I mean I wonder, what will become of us? What will we be called? Are we even part of 'our' generation, anyway? Most of the time I'm vaguely shamed by it — its music, its shitty films. I mean, I hate the Oscars. I'm a mainstream kid. I read a pome in one of those Oxford mags, it was a nice little pome like Ted Hughes without the animals. (Those tears will not travel.) We should refuse participation — absolutely; and in the remit of the pome an arena be opened where I can air my grievances, legit. The mainstream is the real alternative because it is so mainstream, it goes around like a bad joke. Today the Google car went past, I waved. I was out to buy some eggs. It rained, it didn't rain, I mean come on. If we must joust, remember please that I abhor violence in all its forms, metaphorical or otherwise. I have nothing to say to my friends (we all agree) so enemies are the best ones. If only Americans weren't so loud about their feelings, eh? The One Where Joey and Ross Discuss

Poetry. Overall I *liked* your question, the whole vibe and vector of it. I'm upset to not have been plagiarised yet. Resentment is the only thing holding poetry together. We need our Oceania. The biogs are too long and are not relevant to the publication.

Your enemy,

Sam

Date: Tue, 29 Jan 2013 23:12:57 +0000
From: ██████████████████
Subject: Re: collaboration for enemies 2/?
To: ██████████████████

Dear S,

my problems are similar to yours but shifted schematically by a few degrees purely through the un / fortunate reality of chance, as it relates to beginnings, as in enough to know the difference between a real and imagined problem but not enough to have an excuse to be something other than feeling generally well in an attempt to surround myself with a something which is akin to love (or is actually that), which is hard to say, thanks, in part, to the pomes you refer too. and that is an idea of love which is based on knowing what it's opposite is. which is a good way, i have found, to approach concerns like 'generations', 'poetry', 'approachability', as well as love. by the way, are we not friends enough yet for lower case? I've met your ████ and you've met mine (as if we'd be married at our age, generationally), and lest you forget, I've been to where you live. certainly we're friends enough that I might ask you to be part of enemies, somehow, even if obituaries or ████ poems or whatever isn't quite right for you. there is a significant cache around you at the moment because of your book with faber, you have to suspect i might be attempting to bungle hump your coverage into my book somehow. is it all an exchange perhaps? that would be a naive reading of human interaction (where there is warmth to be found, occasionally often) by the kind of arsehole i often have to deal with who would consider themselves revolutionary and thus not capable of the most basic self awareness. do you know what im getting at? that people assume their cynicism is the final destination, when in

many ways, it is the first stop? a token of something to show my in
/ sincerity - no violence. & I shall, at a later date, plagiarise you with
great care / ease.

your enemy
steve

From: Samuel Riviere ████████████████
██
Sent: Thursday, 31 January 2013, 16:19
Subject: RE: collaboration for enemies 2/?

dear s,

i feel shamed, almost, into seriousness. this was always going to be about whose adjustments were the defter ('faber word'), but to find myself outmanoeuvred so early on by this masterful shift to the intimate address is…disconcerting. or maybe i'm getting it wrong? sometimes i feel as if an early misconception i made has been lying in wait for me for years, and then i feel happy, almost, to renounce everything i've read. but poeits can't be the only ones whose most potent, inclusive fantasy is that of adversity, even if i can't think of anyone else right now who finds it as enjoyable to wring hands by the light of their work at some or other centre of privilege. speaking of which, i passed on your note to my guy at *A Huge Reward for Cunts*. *AHRC* as you know is an inside job…. but could you subscribe to a view that private funds might comprise a writer's winning flaw? just as there's something incorrect always with a poeit's appearance (see ████████████████'s nosering), so a personality does its best to counterfeit the text. perhaps this is where the love comes in you speak of — i forgive ████████ and ████████ their ██████ t-shirts and suit jackets over jeans even as i love them for them. there needs to be a uniform or something (there is). ██████ might have been cute, but i admit i feel more comfortable knowing that the eavesdroppers of these missives are notional for the time being. like you said about my stuff on one occasion, to keep it concrete seems appealing (thnx m8) and the fragmentary only vouches for its opposite, don't you find (and don't you like it)? i don't know steven,

sometimes i just think: new zealand. don't be written. my 2nd book is a guide of how to deconstruct my 1st, an apology to the readers and an indictment of the fans. then again, i forgive an ok review i got. i find myself unsure of where to stand. anyway — can we welcome every uninvited reference as if it was their birthday yesterday. i want the guys across the hall to come and spike the punch. i'll b there 4 u, cuz ur there 4 me 2.
your enemy,

sam

Dear S,

Well that's always the risk of being clever, that someone else might use dumb kindness or violence to undermine you. And there's always a chance they're just being manipulative (I refer to the *kindness* of course, the kind of manipulation that occurs in violence is more ... chiropractic), which forces you to be cleverer still. Until that becomes politics, which might be an apropos topic of discussion for us, as poets? Maybe not. I actively seek surgery on that topic, hoping that annulment will come (subjectively of course, not objectively - there'll always be dickweeds involved every thing that is a ███) through my refusal to acknowledge its gryst. Like when a group of children in the street call me a cunt and in a sense, offer me a huge reward, that I might be able to mill through them, and I simply ignore them, and drink my ginger beer. Anyhoo, I have hardly outmanoeuvred you, I can barely tie my laces, all is still in play. I should've mentioned earlier that I've been reading Hobbes, Leviathan, because I don't read newspapers and I wanted to read something that felt relevant to the activities of the Real politics of the country at the moment. But back to poetry, I caught the bit about the tight t-shirts and the jeans and suit jacket (the paul mccartney on top gear) and I now come to see how we differ and where my advantage might lie not that I have come to the point of recognising that love that I evoked in the first missive. My instinct is absolutely not to forgive those who are beautiful because of their incorrection, but rather to instruct, which is not to say I want to make them better, just to offer a new opportunity for them, and that's like an itch. I'm like Carl Jung in dangerous method. Instruction, once, for me, meant physical correction. So you can see now, precisely because I love to hear that is why you love them, and aspire to have that feeling too, there is somewhere for me to grow into. For you, and forgive me for saying so, perhaps the direction of the change / growth is in, like a hair shirt, no more or less important, but with a smaller space in which to wriggle. Which is perhaps why your next book is about your last book, which was a good book, and my next book is about anti-semitism. Perhaps I need to add an addendum to that book which asks, if an incident is witnessed electronically by eavesdroppers who do nothing to prevent its being then ... I've lost my train of thought, anyway, don't worry about the other stuff. You and I are Gatekeepers. Where is Belfast at the moment?

sincerely your enemy
steve

From: Samuel Riviere ████████████████████
██
Sent: Friday, 1 February 2013, 18:22
Subject: RE: collaboration for enemies 2/?

Dear S,

I can see you're trying to help me out of this, in your way. I don't believe I'm capable of instruction, voluntarily, though, except through a dumb willingness to enter further states of confusion... isn't disorder the thriving of actual life? Brian Cox says this sort of thing though I imagine he's high most of the time. I s u p p o s e (?) I envy this ability to command, corral and deploy that I identify in many practitioners, a usage that makes the world seem to fall together or come apart as they see fit. There isn't a second collection. I'd hate for you to think that it was actually that! But I can see how one draws strength from a private knack, one to offset theoretically — or chiro-practically — against one's friends and interests. My favourite thing to do right now is watch a poeits face as they're being introduced at readings, and their plaudits congregate embarrassment. They don't know what to do with the face! That hair shirt, as you so corporeally put it, abrades the spirit in these minutes. The more the zoom is clicked the more itchier it gets, I think. At what point does pride, I don't know, pixellate. I've fallen back a few times (or more) on your own statement that these motives for a pome already seem suspect. But maybe here's a thought, resistance so discrete that no-one notices it. Is this politics, what do you think? Can passivity be the real McFake? It's a genuine question. "You'll write about it here," a friend from here has threatened, but I think not. I have a position, in that I'm alive and sort of awake. I wish I was more admiring, much, but that's my deficit, not one of anywhere else. As always I am touched by your efforts and have much to thank you for. To misquote Chandler Bing, could I be any more direct? I'm not at all cynical, just gullible enough sometimes to believe this stuff. Where will it end, Steven? Maybe something good leaks out. We will disagree with everyone eventually.

Your friend adversarially,

Sam

From: Steven Fowler █████████████████████
To: Samuel Riviere █████████████████████
Sent: Friday, 1 February 2013, 18:35
Subject: Re: collaboration for enemies 2/?

Dear S.

Rarely am I accused of helpfulness. But then you are atypical, which is a compliment, and I should not be surprised. Thank you. And yes of course you're beyond direct instruction, but clearly suggestions occur to us as ideas in the future, dressed in underwear that we imagine is our own. I am laying down brain cement in the hopes that one day your foot get stuck. Isn't Brian Cox an actor? The original Hannibal Lector, in the amazing Michael ... I forget his surname, that director who did Last of the Mohicans, he did the original Thomas ... I forget that author's surname too, genuinely, I'm not being flippant with my forgetful. Harris maybe. He did the original adaptation and it was good, with the guy from CSI. The new Hannibal is Mad's Mikkelsen, which is exciting. A private knack I shall eat by the bowlfull when it comes time to find it free on the internet, when I should be writing a second collection. You strike me as owning the right amount of passivity for your politics, along with the right amount of vitriol. But perhaps there's me rationing out motion as if I could do so easily. It needs to feel that way if you have experienced the lack of control to the point of matter disintegration at your own hands. Definition by opposite again. And there's much to appreciate in your kind words, which are heavy on me, and embarrass me. I can assure you, there is already good leaks all over the place, people can hardly keep it in. Like the supposition of conspiracy, the idea that bad poetry abounds suggests that humans can keep a secret, which they fucking well can't. So out it dribbles, one killing ten, if such numbers should exist, which they don't. Good to hear Belfast is still in Ireland.

Your enemy,
Steve

From: Samuel Riviere █████████████████████
To: ███████████████████████████████████
Sent: Tuesday, 5 February 2013, 12:45
Subject: RE: collaboration for enemies 2/?

Dear S,

I can see you now; I can sort of make you out... This business of disintegrating you speak of makes me remember how I've stopped, before, in summer, on the street, to squeeze the shit out of a *pain au chocolate*. A man barged into my backpack — I was examining, with a heavy heart, the menu outside a certain south London patisserie — and I called him a prick. '*You're* a prick,' he responded, 'Wanker,' said I; 'You are,' was his retort, but he was by now nearing the corner. It was then I clutched the pastry with the force chosen by my feeling. I told you it wasn't a nice story. The Brian Cox I mean, scientist and television personality with grey 'flecks' in his hair, would appreciate, as an enthusiast of material reality, that it matters less what I thought about as I crushed the croissant, than what I paid for it. This seems to mean it matters less what books I've read than it does what books I've bought. This, in turn, makes me feel (un) happily like a frictionless pipe for money to swoosh through, which is another way of saying I feel, failingly, like an attempt at money. Money likes to make its holes look nice. Poeits are perhaps the least fluent in doublethink anyway, so does all this distance just let the stakes keep lowering? I have to go in a minute, Steve, as I'm expected at a birthday party. It's hard to tell how real it is. I think of Roman Polanski, for instance, reclining on a low sofa near an artificial fire. He's probably been skiing! The wind whimpers at the windows but Roman ignores it. Evolution is a mean way to think.

Your enemy,

Sam

Date: Sat, 9 Feb 2013 16:14:19 +0000
From: █████████████████████
Subject: Re: collaboration for enemies 2/?
To: █████████████████████

Dear S,

Technically a Polanski? Illegal-ish? 13 years of age. Obviously because
I am not organically able to produce the appearance or sensation
of being concise, I sometimes wish I could. Whenever I attempt to
do so the impression I give is that I am being physically humorous,
which is not necessarily something I am against, having observed it
deployed with some success by Jack and others. But I am not light or
agile or dappled, as some have described you. But that seems silly to
me, as I know you in real time, you are contemporary to me, and not
a historical figure, like a past advert. Even there in that sentence I am
being clumsy rather than concise. Once in a pub many years ago a
man said to me I was the least ██ person he had ever met, which gave
me pause for thought at the time. I didn't find it amusing at all. I was
open to having a relationship with a man, but that's not really what
he meant. He was saying I am not concise. This is leaked over into
the books I think. What is it like having one book that everyone (you
know) knows? Perhaps the possibility of being flippant, the flirtation
with flippancy, allows room for privacy, though some would say
that is unpleasant, repugnant even, part of an almost calvinist select
of performers and poetry lovers and professional audience members.
But I can assure us both the alternative comes with responsibility.
Like if someone were to pinch you in my company I would be almost
concretely bound to return that pain to them, not to protect anything,
but just because that space which prevents me being seen as concise
is filled with a putty like substance that feeds on a very social form

of chiropracticality. I recently (and this is true) frog marched a man off a bus as he was grabbing the arm of a woman he didn't know and shouting. She screamed for help, her name was Tamarin, and this was at 8.45 on a tuesday or something, going into work, and for a lull moment, no one did anything. I was sitting three rows back, and he wasn't Bananas, or dangerous, just a bit drunk. I got up and thought about beginning a dialogue with him, but in the end was so tired of this responsibility I just grabbed his wrist, turned his arm behind his back and applied a crossface chickenwing. He gave in, sagged like a pouch, and I took him down the stairs and off the bus. He was quietly concise as the bus drove away and then one step later the bus driver told me to get off for fighting. I am Polish? We all have our conflicts.

Your enemy,
Steve

From: Sam Riviere █████████████████████████
To: "steven █████████████████" <steven█████████
Sent: Tuesday, 19 February 2013, 14:20
Subject: RE: collaboration for enemies 2/?

Dear S,

I imagined you dressed in a monk's cowl for the entirety of the last anecdote: a good look for you, I think. Over the course of your email I have, mistakenly I'm sure, equated flippancy with concision. But there's an urge revealed here that perhaps the book has heightened, a tendency almost, and I suspect it is to do with making room for privacy, a small tank to swim in, from which I can press either my face or my arse to the glass — thick enough so the pale shape is hard to greet correctly. I quite often, for instance, pretend I haven't read things when I have: it gives me a luxurious, spacious feeling, like waking up at 10.40am. I never claim the opposite. Hardly ever. Like the way I won't reply to emails or texts immediately, but allow a time frame in which to let a response 'happen', somewhere between a 'Yep' and a 'Ya'. Just imagine if this laughable compulsion were extended to money! Only I think that it might be. I'm refusing autocorrect cues when writing this, more time-consumingly, to give myself the illusion of spontaneity. Being concise is necessarily to be misleading, I might explain your aversion that way. I imagine a street magician or an arsehole like that to be very concise. Talking about this makes it worse, but it lets me feel that cross-face chickenwing more pressingly, more chiropractically. It's the sensitive bristles that I appreciate most about your story, the way it keeps itching, with that unamusing comment you received. These are special discomforts; perhaps they are strictures and it's good to have them pointed out and tugged at: then we laugh. Still, why come to a poem if you're only after one thing. It goes without saying, to quote 19 yr old Californian poets who 'fucking hate' capitalism, that there's something well-lubed about the path of medium friction. I'm starting to understand how we only guarantee ourselves a little more space to swim in, and further product(ion) (more rubbing). Is it even a relief if 'healthy' dissent displays this sort of fluency? I never feel as certain of the 'impossibility of alterity' than when I'm reading that quote about Marx and horizons. Well in any case it's a Gryffindor win — 1000 points to everyone. Forgive the grammar and spelling, this sent in haste from my iPhone.

Yr enemy,
sam

Bear

w/ Samantha Johnson

yep my pent robs the word. History's pressed flower
until that rotating protection of a brush
who teaches / we arent the damned, nor near it
you arent my son / for you are more &
for us there is a courtesy superior to love
& at that I have learnt love / thanks

Saint Augustine of Hippo
w/ David Kelly

for l.d.

Sloth poses as the love of peace
        Saint Augustine

I must carry my thoughts
back to the abominable things I did in those days
the sins of the flesh which defiled my sould
I do this, L., not because I love those sins, but so that I may love you
for love of your love
I shall retrace my wickedness
the memory is bitter
as was the taste of human ear
the fleeting glance of a mongrel dog
as was the taste of the woman's member
but it will help me to savour your sweetness
the sweetness that does not deceive
but brings real joy & never fails
for love of your love I shall retrieve myself from the havoc of
disruption
which tore me to pieces
when I turned away from you*
whom I alone I should have sought
& lost myself instead
on many a different quest

    *though I did not know you then & could nor have known you
     still! salvation out of reach
    is damnation at hand — I ate
    who I ate, & let blood ripple from my chin like plasma

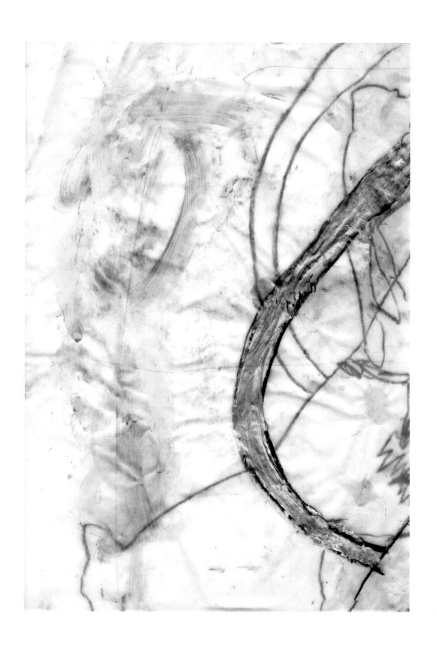

for as I grew to manhood
I was inflamed with desire
for a surfeit of hell's pleasures — cork, concrete
seepage

what light I had seen
that only a crack had let within?
foolhardy
fortnightly

I ran wild with lust that was manifold & rank
in yours eyes my beauty vanished
& I was **foul** to the **core**
though you would *never lend* words
                    to your judgement
yet I was *pleased* with my own condition

& anxious to be pleasing in the eyes of women

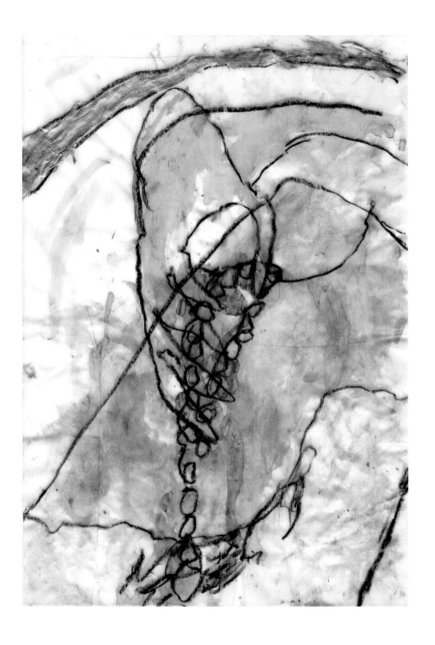

I care for nothing but to love + be loved
but my love goes beyond the affection of one mind for another

beyond the arc of the nightness of friendship
I lied!

bodily desire — in globulus ERNST sharped Morass
& adolescent sex, the desire to savege / pillage / spite / spit /
                                        cluster

welling up within me exuded mists which clouded over
& deceived my heart

so that I could not distinguish the clear light of true love
for the murk of lust

love + lust together seethed within me
in my tender youth they swept me away over the precipice of my
                                        bodies appetites

& plunged me into the whirlpool of sin
more + more, I angered you. Unawares.

but you are not angry!
forgiveness bathes me like breastmilk

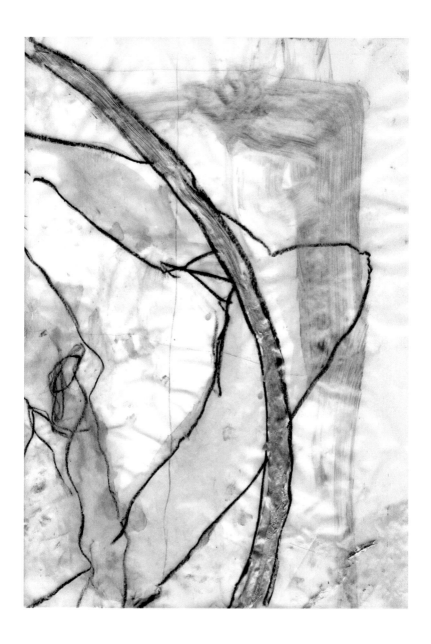

I am your weak limp
    cat — lover & hero
        somewill one when I am dead
           as I take pleasure in their own passing
          I believe in our collaboration
             if kindness will be unkind
       a man whose sense of pity
     was true + sincere
    might want others to suffer
  so that he could pity them
sorrow may therefore be commendable
& so lurks the monster
of my departure
  though who knows if might
     even blink? It is powerless
    to stab you, L.

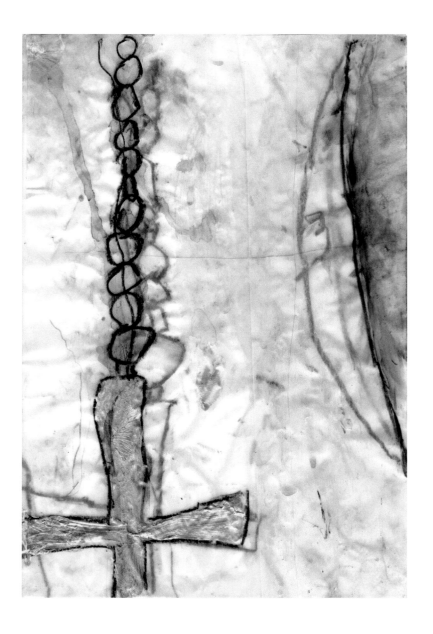

I imagined a man and a woman copulating and I was disgusted because their union might produce life

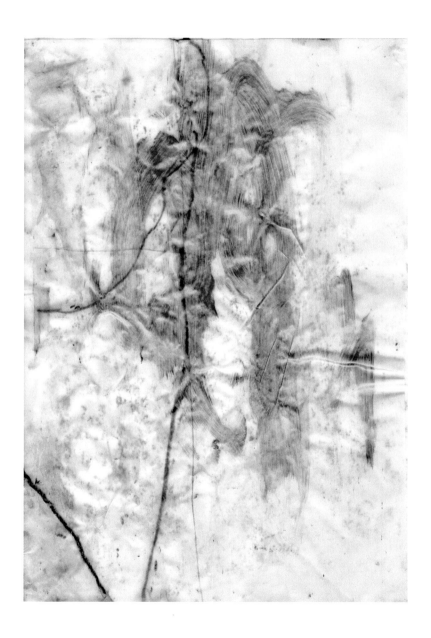

for maintenance of the critical spirit
that can say No and act without puncturing
the delicate membrane of its Yes

mine body - thou maketh me sad - mine soul
thou maketh me brave   but   alas   I have no wings
no wings - thing - body stayed poor in childbirth
I weakened thee with my seede
now thou art weake
thou art supple
hast thou teeth? - bite onto the flesh of mine seede
seest her nosebleed? how crimson runs

now that it has come to close
my boyish confidence
has been replaced
by a man's cruelty
the endless quality

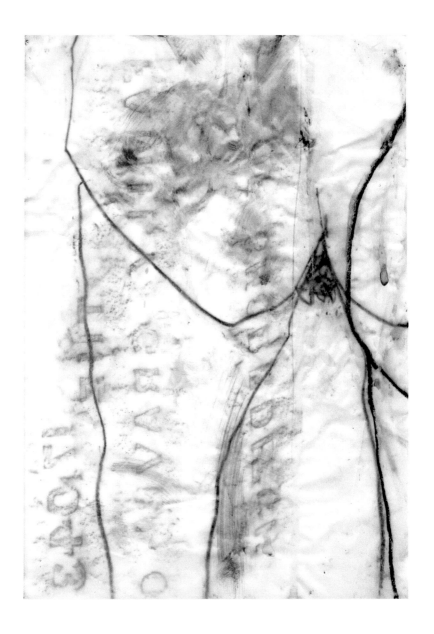

NOTES

The Mechanical Root...... Emily Critchley

A poem to celebrate the birth of a first child, written in block exchange.

Museum of Debt...... Alexander Kell

The Museum of Debt is an exploration of the unspoken in a contemporary British workplace — most specifically a workplace where the task in hand is the preservation of dead objects — inanimate historical trinkets which pass on their own ossification to their watchmen & watchwomen, and breed a myriad of depressions. Between the concussion of photography and irony of poetries, so the Museum of Debt is about mortality, and a mild form of waking death. Both poet & photographer involved were doing the job they documented. A project of internal projection with an innately shared set of meanings and experiences. (A selection from a larger work previously published, in part, by OFI Press.) *alexanderkell.com*

Gilles de Rais...... David Kelly

An interchangeable narrative reflection on the life and legend of Gilles de Rais, this fusion of avant-garde poetry and modernist line drawing aims to satirise and subvert the manner in which the monstrous myth surrounding de Rais is echoed in our own time by Jimmy Saville. This is the disjunctive folklore of idiots resounding through the ages, from 15th century France to 21st century Britain. (A selection from a larger work published in its entirety as postcards, double-sided with image and text, loose-leafed in a book in a box, by Like This Press in 2013.) *erkembode.com*

Ways of describing cuts...... Sarah Kelly

"Aiming to surpass the benign conversational format of much poetic collaboration, these poems aim instead to arise from a violent and impulsive sort of play... The poems appeal to each other as much as they aim to appall, teasing, correcting and provoking, meeting each other's lunges with unexpected gentleness." Sam Riviere (A selection from a larger work published in its entirety by Knives, Forks & Spoons Press.) *s-kelly.co.uk*

Art Gallery Bouncer...... Patrick Coyle

An exchange of aberrant found text exploiting the language of the internet and spam emails, the source limitation is intended to provide a direct link between the author's selections and their own poetic intentionality, and to formulate a cogent narrative through unexpected overlaps. (A selection from a larger work that was published in its entirety by Gauss PDF, 2011.) *patrickcoyle.info*

Animal Husbandry...... Sian Williams

The inkblot test (also known as the Rorschach Test) is a method of evaluation psychologists use to examine the personality characteristics and emotional functioning of their patients. This test is often employed in diagnosing underlying thought disorders and differentiating psychotic from non-psychotic thinking in cases where the patient is reluctant to openly admit to psychotic thinking. (A selection from a larger work published in its entirety as a limited edition pamphlet by Kitt Press in 2010.)

40 feet...... David Berridge

A large scale, free-flowing dialogue poem broken into many modes and fragments that aims to encapsulate a very specific moment in time — London now, in 2012 / 2013 — and all its events, happenings, environs and languages, in order to fix the subjective, the miniature, the specific through an open ended totality of expression. Written first in poem exchanges, and then opened up to larger writing blocks, re-formed and re-edited. (A selection from a larger, 40 poem work.) *davidberridge.wordpress.com*

The Rasenna...... David Kelly

Collage poetry, deliberately designed to be a disjunctive and elegiac mocking of contemporary notions of historicism, mythical art veneration and the 'lost' works of pre-modern civilisations. (A selection from a larger work that was rendered in collage and in image / poem format. Published in part by Rattle Magazine and exhibited at My Pixxa, London, 2012.) *erkembode.com*

Secretum Meum...... Tim Atkins

A rewriting of the Petrarch text which sees a dialogue between the young Petrarch and Saint Augustine. The work takes on the form of the dialogue in classic philosophy, subverting its antiquated form to a contemporary, awkward vernacular. An extension of Tim Atkins' remarkable, ongoing Petrarch translation project.

1000 Proverbs...... Tom Jenks

The intention and expectation of the Proverb form twisted, reappropriated, and often just dumped on, '1000 Proverbs' is a rapid fire exchange in the realm of the absurd / wise. *zshboo.org*

Cannibals...... Ilenia Madelaire

Minimalism in poetry meets maximalism in illustration. *ileniamadelaire.com*

Panopticon...... Hannah Silva

Jeremy Bentham's prophecy rendered poetic, an exchange of stanzas exploring the overseeing eye. *hannahsilva.wordpress.com*

Battles...... Ross Sutherland

Possible future tour ideas. *rosssutherland.co.uk*

Inside the Actor's Studio...... nick-e melville

A unique enmity and love pours north and south over Hadrian's Wall; as with every overfamiliar relationship, depth and despair come together. Unchecked splurges and utterances exploring psychosis, alcohol, violence and the coming doom.

Brumhold's diary...... Lone Eriksen

A parody of classic European realist fiction and the Scandinavian / Habsburg fin de siècle era, the deliberately distorted images of people taking pictures are linked to an excerpted diary. A tiny glimpse of what might seem like a massive narrative and one that carries with it the tonality of the detail, introspection and excessive information of the 'great' novel. Brumhold is actually a character in Walter Abish's novel *How German is it?* (A selection from a larger work previously featured, in part, in Rattle Magazine.) *loneeriksen. com*

The Revenge of Miguel Cotto...... Philip Venables

Born of the London Sinfonietta's Blue Touch Paper programme, which aims to instigate and promote a new generation of composers and inter-disciplinary collaborators, this piece aims to explore the notion of violence within boxing through music and avant-garde poetics, and retelling the real life story of Miguel Cotto and Antonio Margarito. An excerpt was premiered at the Village Underground in 2012, and performed again at LSO St Luke's in 2013. Reprinted with kind permission of University of York Music Press Ltd. *philipvenables.com*

Videodrome...... Claire Potter

Taking YouTube's call and rehash methodology for production, Videodrome collects the poetic responses of the authors as they alternately drift through the video archive, dredging up challenges for each other to respond linguistically to the moving images.

a Recipe for Franglais...... Frédéric Forte

This recipe was concocted using the constraints of the Mathews corpus, using only words that exist both in English and in French, with different meanings in each language. See the *Oulipo Compendium* for further details. (This poem featured in *Recipes*, published by the Red Ceilings Press 2012.)

a Recipe for Hákarl...... Eiríkur Örn Norðdahl

Hákarl or kæstur hákarl (Icelandic for *shark*) is a food from Iceland consisting of a Greenland shark or sleeper shark (*Somniosus microcephalus*) which has been cured with a particular fermentation process and hung to dry for four to five months. Hákarl is often referred to as an acquired taste and has a very particular ammonia-rich smell and fishy taste. Hákarl is served as part of a *þorramatur*, a selection of traditional Icelandic food served at *þorrablót* in midwinter. It is readily available in Icelandic stores and is eaten year round. (This poem featured in the collection Recipes, published by the Red Ceilings Press 2012.) *norddahl.org*

Elephanche...... Marcus Slease

As poet and scholar David Buuck said, 'Some poets can write good plays, but most cannot and should not. If a poet writes a great play, it should not be Poets Theatre, but should be in a book instead.' *Elephanche* is made up of textual/language centred plays and not poet's theatre. They are plays and they are poems. A poem as a play that'll never be performed, at least as a play for actors, perhaps. (A selection from a larger work published in its entirety by Department Press, 2013.) *marcusslease.blogspot.com*

Dead Souls Like...... Chris McCabe

A shape shifting ode to the (best?) city on the earth, where people are the (kindest?) harshest people they can be, given their mood, and circumstance. An exchange born of personal affiliation and biographical weight, it skews and renews the self-referential nostalgia so central to the place it speaks of with alacrity and fondness combined. Blaise Cendrars' *Prose of the Trans-siberian & of the Little Jeanne de France* looms over a kind of Scouse-Cubism while a curious tension develops between latent anger (Fowler) and a sense of the city's ludic and tragic history and subsequent re-blossoming in the 21st Century (McCabe). *chris-mccabe.blogspot.com*

Inner life of Man...... Anatol Knotek

A play or a translation between visual and lingual poetry, and back again — between English and German, between discussion and representation. The interplay between the texts and visuals strains to achieve equality, and in such fruitful tension the work sits, achieving its aims. (A selection from a larger work previously featured, in part, in *The Dark Would,* ed. Philip Davenport, and AAA Magazine.) *anatol.cc*

The 'Burbs...... Ryan Van Winkle

Poems written in block exchanges and then through-written about cityscapes whose culture has somehow shaped the authors. These poems also aim to document the positive cross-pollination of literary poetry with more avant-garde linguistic disjunction. *ryanvanwinkle.com*

you'd love me, I'd tell everyone...... Cristine Brache

Calling cards for escorts, a work for the potentially Lonely that draws on the special, undramatic ennui that sex and the sex industry can produce as a sort of bi-product slug trail when offering 'relief'. These works of photography / art / collage / poetry celebrate the grimy real of the blind pursuit toward love. *cristinebrache.info*

Phänomenologie mit einigen geist...... Monika Rinck

A prose poetry collaboration on the borders of two languages that profanes the good sense of both. Disjointed theft from philosophy and 'classic' literature fuses with the intensive avant-garde poetry of the 21st century city, Berlin and London respectively in an attempt to push the squalid and incommunicable past the pristine and neat. (A selection from a larger work previously featured, in part, in *SAND*: Berlin's English literary journal.)

Muyock...... Matteo X Patocchi

A collaboration about beauty & sexuality, & its idiosyncratic constitution, against homogeneity and the contemporary consumption of the aforementioned. The tradition of classic central European art / fashion photography meets the tradition of central European modernist poetics and typographical innovation. *matteopatocchi.com*

Long letter, Short farewell...... Sam Riviere
An explanation of the work is in the work. *samriviere.com*

Bear...... Samantha Johnson
Posthumous familial thank you letter / portrait of a younger poet.

Saint Augustine of Hippo...... David Kelly
An exchange about the circularity of sexual passion and love at the heart of the work of St Augustine, using found excerpts and rewriting techniques placed alongside an immense, grotesque portrait of the back of a naked Augustine put through jigsaw surgery. The portrait is divided into small sections to be reassembled in the mind. A work lamenting the profound legacy of Augustine's horrifically damaging neuroticism that takes him so far from his own ideal that it returns him to a pure sort of love — discovery. (A selection from a larger work published in its entirety as a limited edition pamphlet by Kitt Press in 2010.) *erkembode.com*